Phonemic Awareness

A Step by Step Approach for Success in Early Reading

Idalia Rodriguez Perez

ROWMAN & LITTLEFIELD EDUCATION

Lanham • New York • Toronto • Plymouth, UK

Published in the United States of America
by Rowman & Littlefield Education
A Division of Rowman & Littlefield Publishers, Inc.
A wholly owned subsidiary of The Rowman & Littlefield Publishing Group, Inc.
4501 Forbes Boulevard, Suite 200, Lanham, Maryland 20706
www.rowmaneducation.com

Estover Road
Plymouth PL6 7PY
United Kingdom

Copyright © 2008 by Idalia Rodriguez Perez

British Library Cataloguing in Publication Information Available

Library of Congress Cataloging-in-Publication Data

Perez, Idalia Rodriguez, 1940-
  Phonemic awareness : a step by step approach for success in early
reading / Idalia Rodriguez Perez.
    p. cm.
  Includes bibliographical references.
  ISBN-13: 978-1-57886-749-3 (cloth : alk. paper)
  ISBN-10: 1-57886-749-5 (cloth : alk. paper)
  ISBN-13: 978-1-57886-750-9 (pbk. : alk. paper)
  ISBN-10: 1-57886-750-9 (pbk. : alk. paper)
  1. Reading--Phonetic method. 2. Reading (Early childhood) 3. English
language--Phonemics--Study and teaching (Early childhood) I. Title.
  LB1050.34.P47 2008
  372.46'5--dc22   2007042965

Contents

Introduction

Over the past two decades or more, but mostly in the last 8 to 10 years, there has been growing agreement about the critical importance of phonemic awareness to beginning reading success. As early as the 1990s, research in early reading brought about a myriad of explanations regarding the concepts of phonological and phonemic awareness. The definitions on phonological and phonemic awareness left many with questions on how or what to teach young children.

Phonemic Awareness is not phonics. Phonemic awareness is an understanding about spoken language. It is the ability to notice, think about, and work with the individual sounds in spoken words. Before children learn to read print, they need to become more aware of how the sounds in words work. They must understand that words are made up of speech sounds, or phonemes.

Phonemes are the smallest parts of sound in a spoken word that makes a difference in a word's meaning. Early readers can show they have phonemic awareness in several ways, including recognizing which words in a set of words begin with the same sound, isolating and saying the first or last sound in a word, combining or blending the separate sounds in a word to say the word, and breaking or segmenting a word into its separate sounds.

Phonemic awareness can be taught and learned. Effective strategies include teaching students to identify a particular sound in a word; recognize the same sound in different words; recognize the word that begins or ends with a different sound from a group of three or four words; segment and blend the sounds in a word; and manipulate sounds in a word through deletion, addition, and substitution of other sounds.

Phonemic awareness helps students learn to read and spell. The most effective instruction quickly moves the student from awareness of a particular sound to an association of that sound with a letter symbol. Once letter symbols are introduced, students should be able to manipulate the sounds within words by using the letter symbols. The best results take place when introduction focuses on one or two phonemic manipulations at a time, rather than three or more manipulations. Several simultaneous manipulations may cause confusion, dilute the teaching of a particular manipulation, or introduce more difficult manipulations before easier ones can be mastered.

Instructional strategies in blending, rhyming, alliteration and segmentation help young children to develop phonemic awareness. These strategies combine playful type of activities with literary pieces that exposes young children to the rhyme and rhythm of our language; exposure to language through poetry and music lead children to play with the sounds of language.

Very often the terms phonemic awareness is used interchangeably with phonological awareness, as was the case during my observations students during their field experience. Although there is no single definition of phonemic awareness, for clarity in this text it will be described as an insight about oral language and in particular about the segmentation of sounds used in speech communication. It is characterized in terms of the facility of the language learner to manipulate the sounds of oral speech. On the other hand, to unlock the differences between phonemic awareness and phonological awareness, the former refers to an understanding about the smallest units of sounds that make up the speech stream: phonemes and the latter encompass larger units of sound as well, such as syllables, onsets, and rimes.

Research findings regarding phonemic awareness are not new to literacy; however, it is only in the recent years that these findings have gained wide attention. For over 50 years discussions have continued regarding the relation between a child's awareness of the sounds of spoken words and his/her ability to read. During the 1940s some psychologists noted that children with reading disabilities were unable to differentiate the spoken words into its sounds and put together the sounds of a word. The decades of the 1960s and 1970s experience a surge of studies by psychologists but it was the research by the reading education community in 1967—"The First Grade Studies"—that hinted at the important relation between sound awareness and learning to read.

More recent studies (IRA, 1998) of reading acquisition have demonstrated that the acquisition of phonemic awareness is highly predictive of success in learning to read, but more importantly, in predicting success in learning to decode. More pointed, phonemic awareness abilities in kindergarten or within that age-range, appear to be the best single predictor of successful reading acquisition.

According to the IRA's position paper (1998), "that phonemic awareness predicts reading success is a fact." The question that emerges, is on why the strong relation exists. An explanation, interpreted is that phonemic awareness supports understanding of the alphabetic principle, an insight that is crucial in reading an alphabetic orthography.

Most researchers advocate that we consciously and purposefully attend to the development of phonemic awareness as a part of the broad instructional program in reading and writing and kindergarten children or younger should have many opportunities to engage in activities that teach them about rhyme, beginning sounds, and syllables. Since different children many need different amounts and forms of phonemic awareness instruction and experiences, the teacher needs to determine the amount of time of instruction needed based on his/her understanding of phonemic awareness and students' needs and abilities.

One thing must be clear from the beginning, we cannot give so much attention to phonemic awareness instruction that other important aspects of a balanced literacy curriculum are left out or abandoned. This textbook is primarily a guide to the development of phonemic awareness as a part of the total language arts school program. The textbook provides teachers with strategies, sample lessons, assessment techniques and resources that teachers need to develop an effective phonemic awareness program.

The textbook is organized as follows: Introduction; Chapter 1—The Sounds of Words: A Theoretical View; Chapter 2—Phonemic Awareness: An Overview; Chapter 3—Questions and Answers about Phonemic Awareness; Chapter 4—Phonemic Awareness Assessment; Chapter 5—Fundamentals of Phonemic Awareness Every Practitioner Should Know; Chapter 6—Instruction and Strategies. The Appendixes include: A—Other Activities to Develop Phonemic Awareness; B—Literary Selections; C—List of books That Support Phonetic Elements; D—Websites on Phonemic Awareness; E—Form letter to Parents in English and Spanish; F—Common Phonogram List.

1

The Sounds in Words:
A Theoretical Perspective

The research in phonological awareness and phonemic awareness has focused primarily on the significance of these two areas to success in reading. Over the past two decades research studies have leaned mainly on the contributions of phonological awareness and to reading acquisition. Stanovich (1986) best explains the relationship between phonological awareness and reading as not unidirectional but reciprocal in nature.

Early reading is dependent on having some understanding of the internal structure of words, and explicit instruction in phonological awareness skills is very effective in promoting early reading. Noted in the research, is the importance of systematic instruction in early reading. Specifically, explicit instruction in letter-sound correspondence to strengthen phonological awareness, and in particular the focus on the more sophisticated area, phonemic awareness is needed to help young learners become successful readers (Snow, Burns, and Griffin, 1998).

There is sufficient evidence that young children in early childhood programs such as, pre-kindergarten, kindergarten, or Head Start can benefit from instruction that teaches them that words are made up of sounds and that those sounds can be moved and changed. The instruction in phonemic awareness continually stresses the awareness that sounds make up spoken words.

Young children are taught to manipulate these sounds early through playful and interactive tasks such as, saying the sound of the letter that begins their name, noting that words rhyme, and hearing puppets who talk very slowly to model sound segmentation. The awareness of sounds is not present in many young children before they enter school, since recognizing individual sounds of letters is not necessary for speaking or understanding spoken language.

LANGUAGE BACKGROUND OF THE YOUNG AND ITS RELATIONSHIP TO PHONEMIC AWARENESS

Linguists, through the years, have found that human infants give their attention to human voices. They listen and respond to human voices, first in babbles then in word sounds (e.g., /d/, /d/, /d/ or /m/, /m/, /m/), and the adult caregiver often interpret babbling as spoken language, and will say, "the baby said, dada (daddy) or ma/ma/ma (mama)". At this early stage infants are producing sounds that correspond to the alphabetic principle.

Soon after, between the ages of 18 months to 2 years, young children realize that everything (objects, people, elements. . .) has a name. Their vocabulary expands very rapidly as they hear more and more words. Important to instruction in phonemic awareness is an understanding of how the language young children have developed before they enter a school setting.

Between the ages 3–5, young children develop speaking ability very rapidly (Beaty, 1994). Children ages 3, 4 and 5 speak in expanded sentences. They begin by saying, "Give me (pointing to) glass water (when in fact they are asking for a beverage, milk, juice, soda)." Later, they may say, "Give me milk", or "Mommy, give me milk". Some children who do not speak in sentences may do so for many reasons: shyness; ill at ease in the presence of others; come from homes where language is not used so extensively; or have a physical or mental impairment (Beaty, 1994).

It is necessary to understand that during the periods from infancy to about age 5, the child has been developing sounds and language in a very non-threatening environment. Parents/caregivers have supported and helped with language development. This language-base is necessary to later support the instruction they will receive in phonemic awareness. Some of the sounds children will learn early in the phonemic awareness instructional program are the very ones they produced as infants.

The difference however, lies in the way the adult caregiver supported sound development. That is, the adult did not stop the infant and said, "The /d/, /d/, /d/ you made is the sound you hear is the beginning sound in the word "daddy". The baby produced the sound in isolation and the adult responded to the sound and provided the label of "dada" or "daddy". The child at home continued to produce sounds with the adult providing labels (words) for the sounds produced. Essentially, this is the process by which the child developed language at home.

It is important to note, that at about ages one and two children use only ten basic sounds. By ages three and four young children use most sounds but have difficulty with /s/, /l/, /r/, /th/ and /sk/. Children ages four through five have usually mastered most of the sounds but may continue having problems with /s/, /l/, /r/, /th/ and /sk/. Between ages five and six most children speak in a mature adult style. However, these sounds prove to be difficult for young children; therefore, once they enter learning centers or school settings, teachers need to devote a great deal of time teaching them these sounds using a variety of phonemic awareness strategies.

2

Phonemic Awareness: An Overview

Many practitioners wonder how to incorporate phonemic awareness in their daily lessons since phonemic awareness is viewed by many as too time consuming. They ask:

- How can I incorporate these strategies into my daily teaching?
- Where am I going to find the time to get the strategies?
- Where am I going to find the resources to teach?
- When am I going to have the time to incorporate them into my daily lessons?
- Why do I have to provide instruction in phonemic awareness if I am already including language development?

Teachers have so many tasks to accomplish with their students daily during the teaching day that they view adding one more task to their already full teaching day as a "not an easy" undertaking. They ask "where is the time I need to do all the preparation phonemic awareness instruction requires?" They wonder how long should this program be and where am I going to fit it in the language arts program? Teachers feel challenged when they are asked to add one more task to their already filled teaching day.

I have designed this textbook with the classroom teacher in mind. My goal is to help the classroom teacher include phonemic awareness strategies in their daily instruction throughout the day without the stress and job of having to spend more hours of preparation time. This resource guide helps them have an understanding of phonemic awareness and the role it plays in preparing young children for reading instruction; it also offers many strategies that can be integrated into the regular language arts curriculum. The text includes already prepared instructional units and lessons with a variety of strategies that can be used to strengthen phonemic awareness for all students in the early grades classrooms, Head Start programs, or Day Care centers. The contents of these units can be spread over periods of time to meet students' needs. The units are not intended to be used as separate from the regular required reading school program but rather to be used to augment the quality of instruction in literacy. It provides assessment strategies and tools to help the teacher monitor students' progress.

All current related professional literature and research highly supports instruction in phonemic awareness as a key element of a quality reading program. To help every classroom teacher teaching young children, the preparation and compilation of strategies and resources to develop phonemic awareness is deemed timely and appropriate.

PHONEMIC AWARENESS: AN OVERVIEW

The awareness that spoken language is made up of discrete sounds is a crucial factor in children learning to read. Some confusion between phonological awareness and phonemic awareness has been noted in the research. Stanovich (1993–1994) defines "phonological awareness" as the ability to deal explicitly and segmentally with sound units smaller than the syllable. Harris and Hodges (1995) and Adams (1990) go on to explain "phonemic awareness" as the ability to hear and manipulate the sounds in spoken words. The difference between the term phonological awareness and phonemic awareness is explained by Snow, Burns, and Griffin (1998) as follows:

> The term phonological awareness refers to a general appreciation of the sounds of speech as distinct from their meaning. When that insight includes an understanding that words can be divided into a sequence of phonemes, this finer-grained sensitivity is termed phonemic awareness. (p. 51)

Phonemic awareness emerges as one of the most important early step in learning to read. It refers to the abilities to hear rhymes and alliteration as measured by knowledge of nursery rhymes; to do oddity tasks such as comparing and contrasting the sounds of words for rhyme and alliteration; to blend and split syllables; to perform phonemic segmentation such as counting out the number of phonemes in a word; and to perform phoneme manipulation tasks such as adding, deleting a particular phoneme and re-generating a word from the remainder (Adams, 1990).

WHY IS PHONEMIC AWARENESS SO IMPORTANT?

Overall, educators are always looking for valid and reliable predictors of educational achievement. One reason why educators are so interested in phonemic awareness is that it is supported throughout the research as the best predictor to success in early reading and decoding, even better than IQ, vocabulary, and listening comprehension. Once beginning readers have some awareness of phonemes and their corresponding graphic representation (graphemes), further reading instructions heightens children's awareness of language, assisting then in developing the later stages of phonemic awareness. Yopp (1992) explains phonemic awareness as both a prerequisite for and a consequence of learning to read.

Cognitively and structurally, phonemic awareness is challenging for many young children. Children in general struggle with phonemic awareness. For most young children having to think (cognition) about the meaning of a word and deal with the form (structure) of the word is an enormous responsibility. Children at this young age have not yet developed the ability to think of the meaning of the word or the form of the word simultaneously. Stanovich (1992) explained that phonemic awareness instruction must focus on the form (structure) of words rather than their meaning. For these reasons, it is important that young children receive instruction that specifically targets the structure or form of the word, that is, that words are made up of sounds; and better yet, focus on words which they are already in their speaking vocabulary and are familiar with.

Phonemic awareness plays a vital role in learning to read because it helps young children make the connection between spoken language to written language. For this reason kindergarten children must have the opportunities to engage in activities that teach them about rhyming, beginning sounds, and syllables (IRA, 1998). Torgesen, Wagner, and Rashoote (1994) maintain that phonemic awareness has a casual relationship with literacy achievement and in kindergarten is the single best predictor of later reading and spelling achievement in first and second grades. This finding supports other research that indicates that knowledge of phonemic awareness is indeed one of the most significant predictors of success in early reading. In kindergarten, phonemic awareness predicts growth in word-reading ability. The related literature points to an explanation of why phonemic awareness is necessary, explicitly, it supports an understanding of the alphabetic principle which is central in reading an alphabetic orthography.

Children with high phonemic awareness outperform those with low phonemic awareness on all literacy measures, whether they are taught using a whole language approach or a traditional basal approach (Griffith et. al., 1992). Regardless of which approach is considered, practitioners presenting a balanced reading approach to reading instruction help children develop phonemic awareness through language and literature-rich activities. These activities are associated also with whole language activities and aim at enhancing meaning, understanding, and love of language with explicit teaching of skills as needed to develop fluency associated with proficient readers.

As beginning readers, young children must first have some understanding that words are composed of sounds (phonemic awareness) rather than their conceiving of each word as a single indivisible sound system. This awareness is not a discrete state, but rather a sequence of development ranging from simple to complex. Practitioners are faced with the difficult task of helping each child to become aware that spoken words are made up of the sounds represented by letters (phonemes) through systematic instruction. Phonemic awareness is much more complex than auditory discrimination, which is the ability to perceive that cat and rat are different words. To be able to describe how these two words are similar but different, implies some level of phonemic awareness.

Whereas, auditory discrimination requires hearing a difference, phonemic awareness demands a level of analysis of each sound in a word. Young children are normally called upon to consider two tasks: (1) that words are composed of sounds at one level and (2) to understand their meaning at another level. Experiences with rhymes are some of the first tasks that help children discover the structure of words.

The mark of the alphabetic stage or letter-name stage is the realization that letters represent sounds (Chard and Dickson, 1999). As students begin to understand this concept, they use initial consonants, then initial and final consonants, and finally all the elements in a word. Since decoding skills have not yet been developed or may be limited at this stage, students rely heavily on picture clues or picture clues in combination with the initial consonant.

A substantial body of evidence has provided insight that knowledge of phonemic awareness is a precursor to success in reading performance. Phonemic awareness in young pre-readers was found to be a better predictor of success in beginning reading, than such factors as age, socioeconomic status and I.Q. (NAEP, 2000).

Awareness is not an antecedent for learning to talk; phonemic awareness is not necessary for speaking and understanding spoken language. However, research shows that given the fact that letters and letter clusters represent phonemes in our alphabetic language, phonemic awareness is a prerequisite for learning to read and later to write. Instructional strategies that focus primarily on the development of phonemic awareness is central in helping students become aware of phonemes in words before they receive formal reading instruction. Teachers will begin to see that phonemic awareness will become more sophisticated as students' reading skills develop (Sensenbaugh, 1996).

Several instructional strategies are similar and may appear repetitious but the intent is to help children have understanding of the notion that words are made up of phonemes (sounds). Phonemes are *abstract* units, this insight is not easily achieved therefore through repetitive strategies and activities young children gain the knowledge necessary to become aware that words are indeed made up of sounds. When words are pronounced, one does not produce a series of discrete phonemes but rather, phonemes (sounds) are doubled into one another and pronounced as a blend. The tasks necessary to help young children develop phonemic awareness include these broad areas: rhyming, alliteration, blending, and segmentation. These areas are developed through specific methods of instruction and an assortment of strategies and materials.

Instruction in phonemic awareness for young children is planned so that at the preschool level, children are engaged in activities that direct their attention to the sounds in words, such as rhyming and alliteration games. Instruction is playful and interactive as children are engaged in rhyming and alliterations games. Instruction engages the children in learning to segment and blend sounds. Segmenting is a more difficult task for young children. In segmenting and blending, the teacher demonstrates segmentation and blending through strategies such as (1) The Rubber Band Strategy; (2) Talking Like a Ghost Strategy; or (3) Saying It Very, Very, Slowly Then Saying It Fast to name a few. These strategies are integrated into the units of instruction as children are presented with challenges in blending and segmentation.

As children develop insight into segmentation and blending, the instruction is planned to combine training in segmentation and blending with instruction in letter-sound relationships. The teacher systematically sequences examples when teaching segmentation and blending as segmentation is a difficult task for most young children. Finally, instruction must be planned so that children learn to transfer what they learn to novel texts and contexts (Spector, 1995).

General recommendation for phonemic awareness activities should follow a playful and interactive style. The tasks are developed through playful and interactive type of activities that encourage children to participate in the learning process. Teachers are urged to keep a sense of playfulness and fun and to avoid drills and rote memorization. Beginning consonants or letter-sound correspondences that are recommended to be introduced first are: s /s/, m /m/, and f /f/. These correspondences are referred to as *continuants* because they are articulated with a continuous stream of breath and are easy to perceive (Gunning, 2000). Use group settings that encourage interaction among children as you first introduce these correspondences. When presenting the sound the letter M makes, have all the children in the class whose name begins with the sound of /m/ come to the front of class.

The teacher goes to the first child and says his/her name making sure that the beginning sound is drawn out, such as /mmmmmmmmmm/ Maggie, /mmmmmmmm/ Mark, /mmmmmm/ Mandy. The teacher continues the same for each child whose name begins with the /m/. Encourage the rest of the children to participate as the name of each child is said. For many children segmenting sounds in words is a difficult task. In teaching children to segment words that begin with the letters p, t, d, b, k and g in which the sounds of these letters cannot be stretched the teacher tries iteration, which means saying the sound several times as in /d/-/d/-/d/- doll. The p, t, d, b, k, and g are referred to as *stops* and cannot be stretched without significant distortion. Demonstrating how to segment words that begin with *stops* through iteration encourage children to interact during the instruction helps them hear the sounds of words or names.

Since the early sixties Elkonin (1963) found that training in phonemic analysis is a useful foundation to beginning reading instruction. The concept of Elkonin Sound Boxes is a strategy that helps children segment sounds in words or names. Elkonin Sound Boxes can be made by drawing three boxes on a sheet of paper or a dry-erase board. The teacher distributes counters to the children. The children are instructed to place the counters above the boxes. The teacher models the activities before the children begin. The procedure follows as, "Say It and Move It". For each phoneme, children move a counter to each box in a left-to-right progression. For example, the teacher says the word *hat*. Children move the counters that represent the sounds they hear in the word hat see Figure 2.1.

Children then say the word again, sliding their finger below the boxes from left to right: hat. The teacher can use Elkonin Sound Boxes with other activities such as listening for the beginning sound in a word, listening for an ending sound in a word, and segmenting sounds in a word. For example, have children listen for the /m/ sound in the beginning of the word, *man* and place a counter in the first box; or place the counter in the middle of the box if you hear the /m/ in the middle of the word; or place it in the last box if you hear the /m/ sound at the end of the word.

Duplicate the practice exercises in Figure 2.2. Direct students to the picture of the sun at the top of the page and ask them to say the name of the picture. Guide them to stretch the sounds they hear in the word represented by the picture. The purpose is for the students to hear the separate sounds. For those students that have difficulty, provide additional demonstrations. As you demonstrate with the word *sun*, say the first sound in the word *sun* and guide them to put a counter in the first box; as they hear the second sound tell them to put a counter in the second box; when they hear the last sound tell them to put a counter in the third box. Have the students continue with the practice exercise as you move to the next picture until all fifteen pictures have been completed. As students' abilities develop in sound-

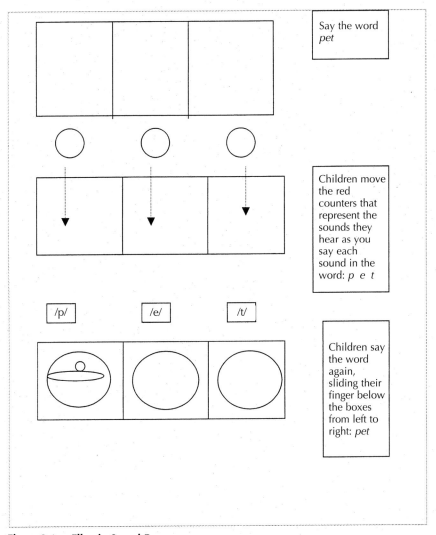

Figure 2.1. Elkonin Sound Boxes

symbol relationships, you can modify this exercise by having the students place plastic alphabet letters instead of counters in the sound boxes as they hear or say the sounds of the words.

Give children only the letters for each word, for example, give them the s, u, n as they complete the first picture in the practice exercise. Continue with this process until all pictures are finished. Assess the children knowledge by giving them the letters a, l, p, s, and n. Have the children place the corresponding letters in the boxes for the phonemes as you say words. For

Task	Example	Ability
1. Rhyming/Matching Sounds	Hearing sounds in words. Detecting rhyme and alliteration.	Teacher can evaluate student's knowledge of phonemic awareness by reading nursery rhymes, such as:
		Jack be nimble, Jack be quick, Jack jump over the candlestick.
		Student is asked which words rhyme (quick, candlestick).
2. Blending	(1) Smoothing segmented sounds provided by the teacher into a word. (2) Syllable-splitting. (3) Sensitivity to similarities and differences in sounds of words.	(1) Teacher provides the segments of a word: /m/—/a/—/t/. Student blends the segmented sounds into the word, mat. (2) Teacher provides the words: mat, cat, Pat Student is asked to split the onset and the rime. /m/ = onset /at/ = rime (3) Teacher presents the following words: rat, mat, cat, fat. Student's attention is called to the onset and the rime of each word. Teacher may ask: (1) What part of the words is the same? (2) What part is different?
3. Segmentation	Understanding that words can be analyzed into a series of phonemes (sounds).	Teacher models with the word "man" and segments the sounds: /m/—/a/—/n/.

Figure 2.2. Phonemic Awareness Assessment Tasks

| 4. Phoneme Manipulation | Add, delete or move designated sounds and form new words or non-words. | Teacher provides phonograms and models sound manipulation as follows:
-at
cat, mat, pat, nat, lat (nonsense word).
-ake
lake, cake, make, fake, gake (nonsense word)
Student is guided to add or delete beginning sound to form new words or non-words with the phonograms. |
| 5. Compare/Contrast | Student can compare or contrast the sounds of words for rhyme or *alliteration.* | Teacher provides examples of beginning sounds, such as /b/ in ball, bat, and ask the students if both words start with the same sound.
Teacher provides examples of final sounds in words, such as /t/ in nat, bat, let, and ask the students if the three words end with the /t/. |

Figure 2.2.   (*continued*)

example, say, "Lap. The cat sat in my lap". Tell the children to move a counter to the first box as you say the /l/; second counter for the /a/ and third counter for the /p/. Later as they develop sound-symbol awareness have children write letters in the boxes as you dictate words. Tell the children, "Spell the word *big*. The big dog barked at the cat". Big: /b/ /i/ /g/. Variations in the use of Elkonin Sound Boxes are to help children segment sounds in words or names and later to develop reading, writing and spelling. Another technique to use Elkonin Sound Boxes with very young children is for the teacher to draw the three boxes in a sheet of paper or cut out three boxes from card-stack paper and give each child a set of three boxes. Instruct the students to place the three boxes at the bottom part of their desk or table. The teacher demonstrates segmenting sounds by stating, "Listen to the sounds in the word *mat*. I am going to say the word *mat* very slowly. When you hear the first sound I want you to move one box to the top of your desk." The teacher demonstrates by moving the first box to the top of the desk as she says the /m/. The teacher says the second sound /a/

and moves the second box to the top of the desk and says the third sound /t/ and moves the third box. The teacher tells the students, "the word mat has three sounds". I am going to say another word very slowly and I want you to move a box for every sound you hear in the next word. The teacher says the /k/ and observes the students to ensure that they have moved one box forward; then continues with the /a/ as the students move the second box; and finally says the /t/ and observes to see that the students have moved the third box. Allow for and be prepared for individual differences. If a child cannot segment the sounds in a word or name, the teacher may provide other types of segmenting activities. Make sure that the tone of the activity is not evaluative but rather fun and informal (Yopp, 1992).

To assist young children to become successful in reading, a number of evidence-based methods of instruction and strategies are offered in the book. Instruction focuses on developing phonemic awareness through a variety of activities such as, rhymes, songs, riddles, as well as other forms of playful-type (e.g., having students come to the front of the classroom as they learn about a letter that begins their name, among others) instruction. These strategies are intended to promote in young children the knowledge that words are made up of sounds (e.g., phonemic awareness). Included are samples of instructional activities with strategies that can be adapted to fit the needs of many young children, including limited English speakers. It also includes how-to-activities, songs, literary resources and websites to reinforce the instruction for student's phonemic awareness abilities. Phonemic awareness instruction is one of the building blocks of the general areas of phonics that prepares young children for the reading and writing tasks in literacy.

3

Questions and Answers about Phonemic Awareness

WHAT IS PHONEMIC AWARENESS?

Plain and simple, phonemic awareness is the understanding that words are made up of sounds. These sounds can be assembled in different ways to make different words. It is also the ability to hear and manipulate the sounds in spoken words. It involves hearing language at the phoneme (sound) level (Yopp, 1992). Once a child has phonemic awareness, he/she is aware that sounds are the building blocks that can be used to build all the different words they hear.

WHY TEACH PHONEMIC AWARENESS?

The importance of teaching phonemic awareness:

- It requires the learner to notice how letters represent sounds.
- It prepares the learner for print.
- It helps the learner understand the alphabetical principle (that the letters in words are systematically represented by sounds).
- It helps children make breakthroughs in learning to decode.

Once children understand that words can be divided into individual phonemes and that phonemes can be blended into words, they are:

- Able to use letter-sound knowledge to read and build words.
- Hear rhymes and alliteration as measured by knowledge of nursery rhymes.

- Perform oddity tasks (comparing and contrasting the sounds of words for rhyme and alliteration).
- Engage in blending and splitting syllables.
- Perform phonemic manipulation tasks (such as adding or deleting a particular phoneme and regenerating a word from the remainder).

Why is phonemic awareness difficult for the young learner?

- There are 26 letters in the English language yet the number of phonemes vary from 44 to 52.
- Sounds are represented in 250 different spellings (e.g., /f/ as in ph, f, gh, ff).
- The phonemes are not obvious and must be directly taught.
- Acquiring phonemic awareness can be difficult because from word to word and speaker to speaker, the sound of any given phoneme can vary for example, for some individuals pin and pen are pronounced differently and for others there is no distinction and only context clues will provide meaning.
- Understanding the logic of the alphabetic principle and to the learnability of phonics and spelling (Snow, Burns, & Griffin, 1998)
- Analyzing the sounds in words is the most important pre-requisite for success in learning to read and write (Elkonin, 1973).
- Requires decentration (Piaget, n.d.) of language. Decentration means having to deal with two aspects of language at the same time such as:
  - ◦ Ability to abstract a beginning sound from a spoken word
  - ◦ Ability to compare the beginning sound of one word to that of another word (e.g., ball, baby)

Also, decentration is a cognitive ability that many five and six year olds have not yet developed. Decentration is the ability to focus simultaneously on several aspects of a problem and young children at the preoperational stage (ages 2–7) are still at the acquisition stage of cognitive development. According to Piaget (n.d.), this cognitive ability requires "decentration". Decentration underlies the stage of concrete operations which means that a child must be able to deal with two aspects of a situation or problem at the same time. In language, it means that the child must realize that cat represents an animal but is also a word made up of sounds (/k/ /a/ /t/).

For many young children, there may be a decentration lag that results in having difficulty noting sounds in words. Some children who perform normally on general language measures are slow to develop decentration ability which in turn results in poor or slow progress in reading. For instructional purposes, the implications are clear, for those children without decentration, the teacher needs to provide additional instruction that includes many experiences to develop phonemic awareness. Supplementary instruction is necessary to afford opportunities for them to think about the form of language (Watson, 1984).

HOW DO WE TEACH PHONEMIC AWARENESS?

It is necessary for teachers to plan instruction to meet the needs of all children. The activities must be fun and take up only a small amount of the total instructional language arts time. Phonemic awareness instruction should be no more than 10–15 minutes per day. Activities have to be developmentally and linguistically appropriate so that all children have opportunities to fully participate. Approximately 20 hours of class time over the school year should be sufficient, however, if you there are children from homes with little or no literacy experiences, an extended systematic instructional program is necessary.

It has been found that small group instruction is more effective when helping students acquire phonemic awareness (National Institute of Literacy). There are many skills in phonemic awareness, with blending and segmentation being the two critical skills that require longer instructional time.

WHAT ARE THE PHONEMIC AWARENESS TASKS?

- There are seven broad areas of phonemic awareness that must be developed through sequenced instruction. These areas are the tasks of rhyming, alliteration, blending, segmentation, manipulation, isolation, and matching. Instructional units include sample lessons and activities that include these tasks.

WHAT ARE SOME OF THE
CURRENT INSTRUCTIONAL PRACTICES?

- Introduce each phoneme one at a time. In Figure 3.1, "High frequency and Lower frequency consonants" you will find the consonants sequence recommended (Gunning, 2000) to begin instruction in phonemic awareness.
- Provide meaningful names of a sound similar to the sound of the phoneme (/z/- buzzing bee).
- Include tongue twisters to help children hear a particular sound ("Nobody was nice to Nancy's neighbor Nick, but he was never nasty" n-obody was n-ice to N-ancy's n-eighbor N-ick).

I. High-Frequency Consonants	Sample Word(s)
s/s/	sat, Sam, song
m/m/	mom, mop, mat
b/b/	ball, boy, bow
f/f/	fat, for, far
r/r/	ran, rope, rabbit
g/g/	go, girl, gum
l/l/	let, low, lamp
c/k/	cat, cot, cut
n/n/	no, Nan, nap
h/h/	hop, hope, hug
t/t/	toy, tall, ten
d/d/	Dan, doll, dog

II. Lower-Frequency Consonants and y	Sample Word(s)
j/j/	jump, joy, jar
p/p/	pup, pop, pony
w/w/	water, was, wall
k/k/	keep, ketchup, keen
y/y/	yellow, yell, yoyo
c/s/	cent, city, citrus
g/j/	gem, gentle
v/v/	valentine, vine, valley
z/z/	zebra, zoo, zucchini
qu/kw/	queen, quiz, quail
x/ks/	
x/z/	xylophone

Figure 3.1.   High-Frequency and Low-Frequency Consonants and y

- The Stretch strategy helps the learner hear individual sounds in a word, examine each sound, and make meaningful connections for each phoneme. Stretching each sound helps the learner deal with each phoneme as it is being sounded, such as mmmmm-aaaaa-tttt = Mat.
- Onset-rime technique targets phoneme awareness and involves direction instruction in segmenting the beginning part of a word, refer to as the onset, and the final part of a word refer to as the rime. Instead of segmenting a word such as cat into its individual components, /k/-/a/-/t/, the learner is taught to hear the beginning sound component or onset and the final sound component or rime, /k/- /at/. This technique is beneficial for later reading and spelling ability.
- Techniques that identify sounds in various positions in words such as initial, medial, final are necessary for the development of decoding ability necessary in the word recognition component of the reading process.

- Techniques that identify words that begin or end with the same sound.
- Systematic instruction that allows for integration of phoneme awareness activities in a meaningful context and in conjunction with the reading approach used in the school program (http://www.literatureforliterature .ecsd.net/phonemic_awareness.htm).

GUIDELINES FOR PLANNING
PHONEMIC AWARENESS INSTRUCTION

- Identify the precise phoneme awareness task on which you wish to focus and select developmentally appropriate activities to engage children in the task. Activities should be fun and exciting; "play" with sounds, don't "drill" sounds.
  - Use phoneme sounds represented by // and not by letter names when doing activities. Remember that one sound may be represented by two or more letters. There are only three sounds in the word cheese: /ch/-/ee/-/z/. You may want to target specific sounds/words at first and practice ahead of time until you are comfortable making them.
  - Continuant sounds such as /m/, /s/, /l/ are easier to manipulate and hear than stop consonants (e.g., /t/, /q/, /p/). When introducing continuants, exaggerate them by holding on to them: rrrrrrrrring: for stop consonants, use iteration (rapid repetition): /k/-/k/-/k/ /k/atie.
  - When identifying sounds in different positions, the initial position is easiest, followed by the final position, with the medial position being most difficult (e.g., top, pot, Setter).
  - When identifying or combining sound sequences, a CV (consonant-vowel) pattern should be used before a VC (vowel-consonant) pattern, followed by a CVC (Consonant-Vowel-consonant) pattern (e.g., pie, egg, red).

Features of successful evidence-based programs:

- Focus on a basic set of individual phonemes, one at a time.
- Activities designed to make each phoneme memorable through playful type of activities rather than "drill" activities.
- Practice finding each phoneme in spoken words or names.
- Integrate "Ladder to Literacy" (O'Connor, Notari-Syverson, & Vadasy, 1998) program.
- Integrate "Teaching Phonemic Awareness" (Adams, 1996).

HOW DO WE ASSESS PHONEMIC AWARENESS?

- Phonemic awareness should be assessed from the beginning of kindergarten through first grade.
- All students should be assessed a minimum of three times per year to ensure adequate progress toward end of year.
- Students identified as at-risk for reading difficulties should be monitored one or two times per month.
- Phonemic awareness skills can be assessed using the following formal or informal measures.

Who benefits from instruction in phonemic awareness?

- All students learning to read, including preschoolers, kindergartners, first graders who are just starting to read, and older but less able readers.
- Beginning readers starting as early as age 4 can be taught phonemic awareness through rhyming activities.
- Kindergarten and first grade instruction includes blending and segmenting of words into onset and rime, advancing to blending, segmenting, and deleting phonemes.
- Learners must be taught to listen to the sounds of language because what we say is not what they see in print.

4

Phonemic Awareness Assessment

Phonemic awareness is a predictor of early reading achievement (Adams, 1991). It is a conscious understanding of the structure of the spoken language (Griffith and Olson, 1992). It is the ability to hear and manipulate the separate speech sounds in words (Hall and Moats, 1999). In alphabetic languages, phonemes are the basic sound units that are represented by letters (Learning First Alliance, 1998).

Research indicates a strong relationship between phonemic awareness and reading success. A kindergarten child who has phonemic awareness will be ready to talk about the sounds that letters represent, on the other hand, a child who has not developed this concept will not understand that letters and spellings represent spoken sounds (Burns, Griffin, and Snow, 1999); Griffith and Olson, 1992). Explicit instruction in kindergarten should begin so that children who do not demonstrate an understanding of phonemic awareness can develop an understanding of the structure of spoken language.

An instructional program for phonemic awareness needs a careful assessment of children's development in this area. Phonemic awareness can be assessed in many ways including formal and informal measures. The teacher assesses informally by noting which children are able to tell when two words rhyme or begin with the same sound or whether they can blend or segment words.

Assessment can take place using group or individual measures. Individual assessment is more time consuming but it yields more valid results. Gunning (2000) developed several assessment surveys to detect ability in rhyming, beginning sounds, and segmentation. The assessment survey forms are designed to annotate a student's responses and are easy to follow and to interpret.

For example, in assessing rhyming, the rhyming sound survey is made up of eight sets of three illustrations. The first set includes pictures of a man, shoe, pan. The student is asked to name the two pictures that rhyme or which have the same sound at the end. If the student is unable to answer or give an incorrect response, the teacher says, "If you listen carefully, you can tell that man and pan both rhyme. They both have an "an" sound. Now draw a ring around the picture of the man and the picture of the pan to show they rhyme. The teacher continues with this procedure during the administration of the remaining sets of pictures.

Lack of understanding of the structure of spoken language leads to reading failure because of insufficient development of phonemic awareness skills (Edelen-Smith, 2003). Assessing for phonemic awareness can be accomplished in several ways. Several activities have been developed to assess children's ability to hear, identify, and manipulate the individual sounds (phonemes) in spoken words. For example, the teacher can have the student identify the first sound in their name; tell the sound they hear at the beginning of the word rat; substituting the beginning sound in can with /t/, /r/, /f/, /m/ or /p/. The Yopp-Singer Test of Phoneme Segmentation (1995) is a reliable instrument the teacher can use to assess phonemic awareness.

The Yopp-Singer Test of Phoneme Segmentation (1995) is a set of 22 words and is administered to students individually. The student is asked to segment each of the words into its constituent sounds.

The Yopp-Singer Test consists of 22 single-syllable words. The teacher says each word orally and then tells the student to say each of the word's sounds. For example, the word "race", the students is expected to say /t/, /o/, /p/. Directions for administering the test are provided (see Appendix G for copy of instrument). Feedback is immediately provided to the student. If the response is correct, the teacher says, "That's correct". If the response is incorrect, the teacher says the word and its separate sounds /t/, /o/, /p/. Only the responses that the student answers correctly are scored as correct. The teacher records the student's attempts as these attempts can provide information about the student's performance. Partially correct responses show that the student has some ability to segment sounds. Gunning (1998), found that the average kindergartner is able to segment eleven of the twenty-two items. Those students who correctly segment most or all of the words are said to be proficient while those that segment only one or two words or none need intensive work on phonemic awareness. The Yopp-Singer Test (1995) is designed to be administered to kindergartners and first-graders, but can also be administered to older students who have difficulty learning to read (Gunning, 1998).

Another way to assess children's knowledge of phonemic awareness is with the five tasks designed by Adams (1991). Adams identified at least five different levels of phonemic awareness in five assessment tasks that can help the classroom teacher in preparing phonemic awareness instruction to meet the needs of young children. The following are the five tasks: (1) Rhyming/Matching; (2) Blending; (3) Segmentation; (4) Phoneme Manipulation; (5) Compare/Contrast. Figure 2.2 illustrates each task and provides assessment and instructional examples.

Teachers of young children can follow or modify Adams (1991) the five tasks of phonemic awareness to assess for knowledge of sounds in words. Within the five tasks young children are provided with a variety of opportunities to develop sound awareness abilities.

Gunning (2000), believes that a program of phonological awareness should be based on the assessment of the student's development in three broad areas: rhyming, beginning sounds, and segmentation. These areas are also the measures of phonemic awareness, a prerequisite for beginning reading.

The Instructional Units and Task models include activities that can be assessed through the use of these assessment tools to develop phonemic awareness in these seven areas: Rhyming, Alliteration, Sound Blending, Sound Segmentation, Sound Manipulation, Sound Isolation, Sound Matching. For example, the activities for teaching the task of rhyming can also be used to assess a student's knowledge of rhyming words.

5

Fundamentals of Phonemic Awareness Every Practitioner Must Know

Phonemic awareness is best described as the conscious and analytic knowledge of sounds. It is a complex process, because young children must be aware that phonemes (sounds) are abstract (they cannot see the sound, they hear it) and that these manipulatable components of the language make up words. Children must be able to think about sounds in words and also have analytic knowledge of the sounds. When a child has only working knowledge of phonemes; that is, is not able to think about or manipulate them, it indicates that he or she is not able to hear the difference between two phonemes or to distinctly produce them. For these reasons, phonemic awareness is a complex process for many young children.

Developmentally, this awareness depends upon the child's inclination or encouragement to give conscious attention to the sounds (as distinct from the meanings) of words (Adams 1991). Therefore, phonemic awareness is having the ability to deal explicitly and segmentally with sound units smaller than the syllable or the ability to be aware that words consist of syllables; namely, onsets and rimes.

The tasks of learning phonemic awareness call for children to be able to deal with the form of the language. Phonemic awareness is the ability to notice, think about, and work with the individual sounds in spoken words. Before children learn to read print, they need to become aware of how the sounds in words work. They must understand that words are made up of speech sounds or phonemes (/k/ /a/ /t/) and that each sound is connected to a symbol (c-a-t).

The ability to abstract a beginning sound from a spoken word and compare it to the beginning sound of another word is a cognitive (thinking) ability. While this ability is yet not developed by many five- or six-year-old children, it is necessary to involve them in a variety of activities that develop phonemic awareness.

WHY THE DEVELOPMENT OF PHONEMIC AWARENESS?

Children's development of phonemic awareness has been shown to help with early reading. Research (Adams 1991; Elkonin 1963; Gunning 2000) shows that phonemic awareness is a predictor of success in early reading performance success. A second-best predictor of early reading achievement is the ability to discriminate between sounds, in particular, those smaller-than-a-syllable speech sounds that correspond to individual letters (/b/) or graphemic units (-at). Adams further maintains that skillful reading is not a unitary skill but rather a whole complex system of skills and knowledge (processing the sound, connecting the sound to the symbol or letter, understanding sound-symbol relationships, and comprehending the sound in context).

Developing phonological awareness must be part of the overall language program. Beginning reading programs that include phonemic awareness instruction have produced better results in children's early reading performance than those that did not. Test results indicate a strong relationship between phonemic awareness and reading performance in the early grades. Children in general will have difficulty with phonemic awareness unless they are provided with a program of systematic instruction.

Evidence-based data shows that the proportion of poor children having difficulty with phonemic awareness is very high, as they usually enter school with less literacy experience (Gunning 2000). These children have not been read to very frequently nor have they been engaged in much word-play or exposed to many nursery rhymes. A systematic program designed to promote phonemic awareness is necessary and children may need extended periods of instruction (Nicholson 1999).

Teachers can help young children acquire phonemic awareness by providing instruction that focuses on the onset and rime in words. The onset is the initial part of a word, whereas the rime refers to the part of the word that rhymes. This form of instruction helps the young learner hear patterns in words; for example, in the word *mat*, the /m/ is the onset and /at/ is the rime. By substituting the onset with /k/, the new word becomes *cat*. On the other hand, by leaving the onset /m/ and substituting the rime /op/, the new word becomes *mop*. It is vital to develop skills in the concepts of onset and rime to help children in decoding, spelling, reading, and writing.

It is necessary that instructional tasks to develop phonemic awareness include identifying initial consonants, identifying individual sounds in words, rhyming words, blending sounds, matching a word or words to a particular sound, and segmenting sounds. Rhyming activities are helpful for children as young as three, since they already enjoy listening to the rhythm of nursery rhymes. Overall, these tasks develop children's phonemic awareness abilities through fun-filled activities that are nonthreatening. The instructional tasks, when presented through literature that children enjoy, strengthen the foundational skills (e.g., rhyming, blending, and segmenting sounds) that lead to success in reading.

To help young children deal with the sounds in words, they need to be involved in several tasks that help them develop conscious and analytic knowledge of sounds. Tasks such as rhyming, blending, sorting pictures by initial sound or ending sound, segmentation, substitution, matching, and reading aloud are strategies to help develop phonemic awareness. Moreover, the purpose of each task is to help the child build conscious and analytic knowledge of the sounds in words. Each of these tasks is explained through a variety of instructional activities and with a step-by-step procedure for instructing children. Examples will be provided to illustrate the application of each task.

HOW CHILDREN BEST LEARN PHONEMIC AWARENESS

Numerous tasks aimed at helping the young child to develop phonemic awareness have been identified. Adams (1991) identifies five areas that need to be developed: segmentation, manipulation, syllable-splitting, blending, and oddity tasks such as presenting the child with a set of three or four spoken words and asking him or her which of the words is different or does not belong.

Gunning (2000) found sorting objects and pictures to be an effective way to teach and practice rhyming. In sorting, children are asked to group objects or pictures whose names rhyme. Objects are more concrete than pictures and less likely to be misinterpreted. For example, display two boxes, one box with a toy cat in front of it and one with a toy goat in front of it. Tell the children that they will be putting the objects that rhyme with cat in the *cat* box, and those that rhyme with goat in the *goat* box. Hold up a hat and say its name, emphasizing the -at pattern. Say, "*Hat* rhymes with *cat*, both have the same -*at* sound, so I will put it in the *cat* box." Once children understand what they are to do, have them sort the objects. It is important to have them name the object, tell which of the two boxes it should be placed in, and explain why. After all the items have been sorted, have the children name the objects in each box and note that all the objects rhyme. This activity is also a good way to assess children's knowledge of rhyming. You can continue to develop rhyming skills by engaging children in sorting pictures.

Recently, we have seen an influx of activities that include nursery rhymes, songs, poems, story reading, and picture sorts by initial and ending sounds. These are fun activities that engage the total child. Through rhyming, children are guided to hear that words have the same rime or ending sound. Modeling with words that are already familiar to the children facilitates the development of blending and segmentation.

Children have a great deal of difficulty with segmentation. Segmentation involves breaking and hearing each sound in a word. One procedure to help them to hear and pronounce the sounds individually is illustration with a rubber band. The teacher illustrates pulling a rubber band as the sounds in a word are stretched out. The stretching of each sound in a word is done very, very slowly, and then the teacher brings the rubber band back to original size, saying the word the fast way. Or the teacher may talk like a ghost, v v v e e e r r r r y y y (very) s s s l l l ow ow ow l l l y y y (slowly). Segmenting is the opposite of blending and is a first step in stretching the pronunciation of words so that each sound is heard separately. Because segmentation is a difficult task, the teacher segments the sounds in a word and the children are invited to blend the sounds and produce the word. Blending is an easier task for children; during a lesson, the teacher segments the sounds in a word and the children help to blend the sounds and produce the word. Segmentation is taught by modeling to the children with the word that has been stretched. The child is taught to blend the sounds in the word during this procedure.

After the children can blend the sounds, the teacher can begin to have them segment the sounds. After children learn to segment sounds, blending and segmenting activities can be integrated by having them say a word by stretching it (taking the sounds apart) and then saying it fast (blending the sounds). The ability to segment is a necessary skill later in decoding written text in reading.

LETTER-SOUND RELATIONSHIPS

Sorting pictures based on beginning or ending sounds helps children understand letter-sound relationships. The teacher can begin by having children sort pictures that start with a given letter. Once they have mastered the beginning letter, the children can work on sorting letters by ending or rime. Sorting reinforces the concept of segmentation and blending.

Reading aloud to children as often as possible is a natural way to get children to become familiar with how language works. The teacher can use books that support phonetic elements. After children have enjoyed hearing a story, they can go back to the book and find words. Books that have repetitive words or phrases (e.g., *Brown Bear, Brown Bear* by Bill Martin) should be read often enough so that children have the opportunity to memorize words or phrases. Reading often to children cannot be overemphasized. The more a child is read to, the more he or she picks up on the language and the rhythm of the language.

Other activities that have been shown to support phonemic awareness development include teaching sound isolation and teaching sound substitution. The task of sound isolation requires that children identify the beginning, middle, and ending sounds in words. For example, the child is asked, "What is the beginning sound in cat?" "What is the ending sound?" "What is the middle sound?"

The task of sound substitution asks the child to identify a word after the beginning sound has been substituted. For example, the child is presented with the following exercise: "The word pig begins with /p/. If I change the /p/ with the /d/, what is the new word?" (dig). These activities are found throughout the phonemic awareness strategies and lessons that follow.

TEACHING METHODS

A program in phonemic awareness should begin with a careful assessment of students' development in this area. Phonemic awareness can be assessed with informal measures to note whether students are able to tell when two words rhyme or begin with the same sound. You can also informally assess students' knowledge of word blending and segmentation. Assessment can be accomplished using group or individual tests. While the individual tests are time-consuming, they yield more valid results.

Classrooms of young children being taught phonemic awareness are likely to be characterized as environments that teach them the awareness of sounds in words through oral language activities such as songs, rhymes, or choral reading. These activities usually run between five and ten minutes and are part of the language arts program. Which oral language activity a teacher uses depends on the strengths of the particular teacher. If the teacher loves rhymes or poetry, the students will be immersed in learning to hear sounds in words in these types of literature. The teacher's enthusiasm is a crucial element of the instructional activities.

In the phonemic awareness environment, the teacher provides children many opportunities to develop sound awareness by reciting nursery rhymes and poems, substituting sounds, naming words that begin with the same sound, and listening to stories. Through these types of activities, children slowly begin to master the varied tasks needed to develop phonemic awareness.

The techniques and instructional strategies in this book develop sound awareness of the high-frequency consonants, lower-frequency consonants, and *y*. The sequencing of instruction is consistent with Gunning's (2000) view of presenting speech sounds ranging from the easiest to the most difficult.

These phonemes fall into the category referred to as onsets. Onsets are the initial sounds that begin words or syllables. Rimes, on the other hand, are the sound patterns beyond the initial sound. More explicitly, rime is the part of the word that rhymes and refers to the *ake* in *cake*, *lake*, or *take* or the *at* in *cat*, *fat*, or *mat*. Figure 5.1 illustrates a list of the most common rimes and lessons designed to develop skill for each of the onsets and rimes.

The high-frequency consonants are also referred to as continuants. Continuants are speech sounds produced by releasing a continuous stream of breath. They are easier to say and to detect in isolation. The sequence is based on the frequency with which the correspondences appear and their estimated level of difficulty (Gunning, 2000). Special attention must be given to teaching the sounds *s*, *l*, and *r* represent, since some children up to ages five to six have problems with these sounds (Beaty, 1994).

TEACHING ONSETS AND RIMES

As soon as the students have some knowledge of the concept of onsets, the teacher may begin to introduce rimes (see Figure. 5.1). The *th* (/th/) and the *sk* (/sk/) consonant digraphs are difficult for some children aged three to six. Particular attention must be given to these children as these sounds are taught. Each instructional session introduces an onset and is accompanied by texts/materials to be used, the focus of instruction, the procedure, modifications, strategies, and an evaluation.

Rime	Word(s)	Rime	Word(s)	Rime	Word(s)
ay	pay, say, way	ing	ring, sing, wing	est	nest, fest, pest
ill	will, till, dill	ap	nap, lap, tap	ink	pink, mink ,link
ip	rip, nip, tip	unk	hunk, junk,	ow	blow, flow, low
at	cat ,pat, fat	ail	nail, fail, pail	ew	new, few, mew
am	jam, Sam, Pam	ain	rain, pain, rain	ore	more, fore, tore
ag	nag, rag, tag	im	him, Tim, Jim	ed	red, fed, ned
ack	back, rack, tack	uck	duck, luck	ab	crab, nab, tab
ank	bank, rank, tank	um	drum, hum, sum	ob	rob, nob, cob
ake	cake, take, rake	eed	need, seed, feed	ock	rock, mock, lock
ine	pine, wine, line	y	by, cy	op	top, mop, pop
ight	night, light, fight	out	shout, pout	in	pin, fin, chin
an	man, fan, tan	ell	tell, fell, nell	ot	Not, pot, tot
ug	mug, pug, jug	ick	pick, lick, nick		

Figure 5.1.   Common Rimes and Sample Words

The teaching of consonants and vowel correspondences are integrated in the instructional session. Modifications to the instruction can begin after the students have acquired some knowledge of onsets. The teacher can extend or modify a particular instructional session by adding one or two rimes. To help the students develop skills in onsets and rimes, the teacher can add appropriate texts or materials and activities from the suggested list found in the appendixes.

The high-frequency consonants that should be taught first are illustrated in Figure 3.1. Instructional activities should begin with these consonants. Sample words are provided and may be used to construct lessons or activities for young children. High- frequency consonant instruction is followed by instruction on lower-frequency consonants and *y*.

Teaching Onsets

The beginning sound in a word is referred to as the onset, while the ending sounds in a word are referred to as the rime.

- Introduce an onset, for example, *b* as the sound /b/ that begins the word ball.
- Show a card with the *b* and say the sound it represents various times.
- Invite the students to do the same.
- Ask the students if they can think of words that begin with /b/.
- List the words on chart paper or the chalkboard and have students say the words with you.
- Read the words several times before having individual students say the words.
- Encourage all students to take a turn reading the words and identifying the beginning sound of each word.
- Introduce a poem or a story featuring the target sound /b/. For example, read the rhyme "Baa, Baa, Black Sheep" several times, pointing to the /b/ in the words throughout the text.
- Ask students to join you in pointing to the /b/ as you read the poem or story. After several readings, invite the entire group of students to read the poem or story chorally.
- Continue with this process with the remainder of the onsets.

Common rimes and sample words are tabulated in Figure 5.1 to aid the teacher when preparing instruction on specific rimes. The tabulated sample words serve to speed up the process and allow the teacher to have the materials and resources beforehand, therefore minimizing the time spent on preparation.

Instructional activity models have been developed to help you teach phonemic awareness in the early grades. These activities are planned to help you follow a sequence of effective and tried-out activities. Most of the activities include rhyming, blending, segmenting, and reading aloud, which gives students the opportunity to hear a phoneme in a variety of ways. They are organized to follow Gunning's (2000) sequencing of phonemic elements, beginning with the high-frequency consonants, lower-frequency consonants and *y*, to high-frequency initial consonants diagraphs, high-frequency initial consonant clusters, vowels/vowel patterns, and low-frequency digraphs.

6

Instruction and Strategies

The instruction and strategies that follow prepare young children in seven broad areas of phonemic awareness: Rhyming, Alliteration, Sound Blending, Sound Segmentation, Sound Manipulation, Sound Isolation, and Sound Matching. Several resources can be found in the Appendices. Along with suggested resources, rhyming literature is included to help provide children a variety of experiences and practices. A list of common phonograms (word families also referred in the text as rimes) is included for your use. Each unit guides the teacher to evaluate children's sounds knowledge by guiding them through several playful phonemic awareness tasks rather than drills. Phonemic awareness instruction is organized first, with the presentation and definition of each of seven broad tasks of phonemic awareness (Adams, 1990) and second with instructional methods and procedures. The tasks that follow describe the task, procedures, activities, suggested resources, and evaluation.

TASK: RHYMING

Description
  Rhyming requires hearing sounds that rhyme in a series of words.

Procedure and Activities
  1. Provide students rhyming pairs and ask, "do these sound the same?" (mat—pat) or different (fat—car)?
  2. Provide students with a series of words and ask, "what word doesn't belong?" (pill, mill, hill, see)?

3. Show students pictures on cards (two cards with pictures that rhyme and one that does not rhyme). Ask students to name the pictures on the cards out loud. Ask them to find the two that rhyme.
4. Snap and Clap Rhymes
   - Begin with a simple clap and snap rhythm.
   - Get more complex as students move along in rhyming:
     i. Clap   Clap   Snap   fall   Clap   Clap   Snap   ball
     ii. Clap   Clap   Snap   hall   Clap   Clap   Snap   small
     Play the following "I say, You say" game:
     I say fat   You say _____.
     I say red   You say _____.
     I say tell   You say _____.
5. Sit Down Game
   - Have children walk around in a big circle taking one step each time a rhyming word is said by the teacher.
   - When the teacher says a word that doesn't rhyme, the students sit down.
     ○ He   free   flea   spree   key   bee   sea   sent
6. Read poems, predictable books, or songs to students.
   - As you read a poem or a predictable book, pause at the end of the phrases and let the students supply the rhyming words.
   - After you read the poem or sing a song together, ask students to identify the rhyming words.
   - Generate other words that rhyme with the rhyming words in today's shared reading.

Evaluation (student behaviors to look for)
- Able to identify words in pairs that rhyme
- Able to supply rhyming words
- Able to find rhyming words
- Able to sing nursery rhymes and songs including playful songs
- Able to play the rhyming games
- Accuracy of rhyming skill

Materials/Resources
Mother Goose's Nursery Rhymes
Dr. Seuss Books
See Appendix B for additional rhymes

Use
- Whole Group
- Small Group
- Individual Student

TASK: ALLITERATION

Description
   Alliteration is the repetition of an initial consonant in consecutive words, creates phrases that children enjoy repeating just to experience the feelings that result from the repetition of beginning sounds, such as those in "Peter Piper picked a peck of pickled peppers. A peck of picked peppers Peter Piper picked. If Peter Piper picked a peck of picked peppers. Where's the peck of pickled peppers Peter Piper picked?" The teacher uses alliterative tongue twisters to introduce and reinforce the concept of beginning sounds.

Procedure
   1. Recite a tongue twister to the students and invite them to repeat some of the lines. Talk about the tongue twister's beginning sounds.
   2. Meaning is important even when the emphasis is on sounds, discuss the meanings of the tongue twisters.
   3. When reciting Peter Piper, bring a green pepper to class. (For other tongue twisters see under Materials Resources on p. 36.)

Peter Piper
Peter Piper picked a peck of pickled peppers;
Did Peter Piper pick a peck of pickled peppers?
If Peter Piper picked a peck of pickle peppers,
Where's the peck of pickled peppers Peter Piper picked?

   4. Sing songs such as a "Willoughby Wallaby". In this song the sounds of the words are changed so that the last word in the first line begins with a /w/ but rhymes with the last word in the second line.

Willoughby Wallaby Wason,
An elephant sat on Jason
Willoughby Wallaby Wobert
An elephant sat on Robert

   5. Naming Objects: Say the name of an object but omit the initial sound. Have students say what the object is and tell what sound is missing.

   Hold a pen, and say, "Is this an –en?"
   Hold a book and say, "Is this an –ook?"
   Hold a picture of a car and say, "Is this an –ar?"
   Hold a picture of a rake and say, "Is this an –ake?"

Continue with this activity with a many words that are familiar to the students. Engaging them in playful but meaningful instruction is beneficial to reinforce the concept of beginning sound in words.

Evaluation (student behaviors to look for)
   Identify the beginning consonant sound in words.

Materials and Resources

The teacher reads the following poem and asks the students to listen for the sound of /b/. Have students raise their hand when they hear the /b/ throughout the poem. Begin reading, teacher participates by raising the hand when the word that begins with the /b/ is read. Continue until the students understand when to raise their hand. Read the poem the second time and encourage participation in identifying the /b/.

Betty Botter*

Betty Botter bought some butter;
But, she said, this butter's bitter;
If I put it in my batter;
It will make my batter bitter;
But a bit of better butter will make my batter better.
So she bought a bit of butter
Better than her bitter butter
And she put it in her batter,
So 'twas a better Betty Botter
Bought a bit of better butter.

*Before reciting Betty Botter bring to class some cake batter.

Follow the same procedure when reading Hillary Hume. Have students identify by raising their hand every time they hear the /h/.

Hillary Hume

Hillary Hume has a hundred hamsters.
A hundred hamsters has Hillary Hume.
If Hillary Hume has a hundred hamsters,
Will you share a room with Hillary Hume.

John Jacob Jingleheimer Schmidt

John Jacob Jingleheimer Schmidt, that's my name, too!
Whenever I go out, the people always shout, "John Jacob Jingleheimer Schmidt".

The Ragged Rascal
Round and round
The rugged rock
The ragged rascal ran.

With this poem, have students tell which words rhyme. Read the poem once and help students identify the rhyme. Read the poem again and have them identify the rhyming words without your help.

Birthday

Apples, peaches, pears, and plums,
Tell me when your birthday comes.

A Sailor Went to Sea

A sailor went to see
To see what he could see,
And all that he could see,
Was the sea, sea, sea.

Dickery, Dickery, Dare

Dickery, dickery, dare,
The pig flew up the air;
The man in brown
Soon brought him down,
Dickery, dickery, dare.

Use

- Whole Group
- Small Group
- Individual Student

TASK: BLENDING

Description

There are many ways to manipulate those smallest units of sounds when we address phonemic awareness, and one of those types of manipulation is blending. Smoothing segmented sounds provided by the teacher into a word is known as blending. Blending is the ability to move these smallest units of sound together in the speech stream. If children can move those sounds together in the speech stream, they have control over them. Blending sounds is an important ability that young children must develop as it corresponds with decoding when reading.

Procedure

In the sound blending task, the teacher produces the sounds that make a word. The teacher provides the segments of the word (e.g., /k/ /a/ /t/) and the students are asked to blend them together (cat). Blending can be made fun and effective by providing children with game-like or sing-song activities.

1. Teacher presents children with isolated sounds and asks them to blend the sounds together to form a word.

2. Teacher models blending by saying, I am going to say the sounds in a word that you know from the Dr. Seuss story I just read, "Cat in the Hat".
3. Listen as I say the sounds, /k/ /a/ /t/.
4. Blend the sounds together and say the word, "cat".
5. I am going to say other sounds of words you may know.
6. Listen as I say the sounds, /k/ /a/ /p/.
7. Blend the sounds together and say the word. You are right, /k//a//p/ are the sounds in the word "cap".
8. Now listen as I say the sounds in another word that you already know, /k//u//p/, blend the sounds together.
9. What is the word? You are right, /k//u//p/ are the sounds in the word "cup".

Continue with this process using words familiar to the children. Read to the children before engaging them in blending tasks. Poems, nursery rhymes, songs, stories are useful materials to give children background experiences with words that are already in their speaking vocabulary.

Evaluation: Student behaviors to look for when teaching the blending of sounds and the test recommended is the Yopp Test.

- Able to identify onset
- Able to identify rime
- Able to blend onset and rime
- Able to identify single sounds in three words (e.g., cat, mat, pat)
- Accuracy of blending skill

Strategies-Materials-Resources

1. Cat in the Hat (Dr. Seuss's)
2. Rubber-band Strategy (I will say the word slowly as I pull the rubber band, You say it FAST as I let the rubber band go back).
3. Ghost Strategy (I will say the word very, very, very slowly. You say it fast). The teacher explains that she/he will talk like a ghost as she will say the sounds very, very, very slowly. Students take turns saying the word fast.

Examples:
Teacher says, "/k k k k k/ - /a a a a / - /t t t t/". Student says, "cat". (hears each sound)
Teacher says, "/m m m m/ - /a a a a t t t t/". Student says, "mat". (hears on-set and rime)
The teacher can continue to focus on words found in Dr. Seuss's "Cat in the Hat".

Use
- Whole Group
- Small Group
- Individual Student

TASK: SEGMENTATION

Description

Segmentation is the awareness that words are made up of individual sounds and syllables. Children must understand that words can be analyzed into a series of phonemes (sounds) or syllables.

Procedure

1. Engage children in "syllable clap". Explain to them that knowing syllables can help them when they read and write. Ask them to clap with you as you say these words:
   - Cowboy   2
   - School   1
   - Dan   1
   - Alphabet   3
   - Wonderful   3
   - Harry   2
   - Dinner   2
   - Television   4
   - Sandwich   2
   - Kay   1
   - Sunshine   2
   - Calendar   3
   - Delicious   3
2. Counting Syllables. Ask your students to count the number of time you clap for each of these words. Continue this exercise by using the children's names. Ask them to clap as each child says their name. Ask them to count the times they clapped for each of their classmate name. For example, John (1); Samantha (3); Sara (2); Tom (1).
3. Syllable Count
   - Have the children clap for each syllable you say using the following words:
     - a. Train   train   (1)
     - b. Car   car   (1)
     - c. Airplane   air plane   (2)
     - d. Astronaut   as tro naut   (3)
     - e. Conversation con ver sa tion (4)

    Begin with one syllable words and build up to words with 2, 3 or more syllables.

4. Single word segmentation
Teacher models with the word "man" and segments the sounds:
   - /m/—/a/—/n/
   - /p/ - /a/ -/n/
   - /k/ - /a/ - /t/
   - /p/ - /u/ - /l/

    Add more one syllable words to help children build a strong foundation in segmenting, blending, and manipulating phonemes.

5. Elkonian Sound Boxes—For this activity prepare cards with a simple illustration along with a matrix that contains a box for each sound (phoneme) in the word. Each box represents one sound and not necessarily each letter. The word you use should be familiar to the children. Hand out a set of 3 cards/boxes to each student. Tell the children that you are going to demonstrate how to use the cards/boxes. Tell the children that you are going to move a box for each sound you hear in the word "pat". "/p/ move one box forward; /a/ move second box forward; /t/ move third box forward. Ask the children how many sound are in the word "pat". Count the boxes, 1, 2, 3. Say yes, the word "pat" has 3 sounds. Now I want you to listen as I say the following word. You move a box for each sound you hear: /p/ - /i/ - /g/. Check to see that the children have moved forward 3 boxes. Ask them to count the boxes they moved. Say yes, the word "pig has 3 sounds and you are correct in moving the three boxes". Continue with the rest of words.

Pig   cat   dog   kite   hat   bat   mat   go

   - Place plastic alphabet letters in a tray. As you say the beginning sound in the word pig, move the letter p forward; say the second sound and move the i forward; say the final sound and move the g forward. Tell the children the letter p stands for the first sound in the word pig; the i stands for the second sound in the word; and the g stands for the last sound we hear in the word pig. Guide the children through the task of pushing corresponding letters for the word pig into the boxes (3 boxes) as you say each sound. Model the process two or three times. Invite the children to say the word by stretching the sounds so they can hear the separate sounds while you move the letters. Ask for volunteers to push the letters into the boxes while you say the word slowly.
   - Provide more examples so that the children can begin to transfer their understanding of sounds-to-letters in words.

- Have the children identify the picture and then pronounce the word very slowly so each sound is clear. The purpose of the exercise is to have children hear and say each sound in the word without distorting the word and to put a letter in each box while saying each sound.
- Ask the children, "what sounds do you hear in the word pig?"
- Ask the children, "how many sounds do you hear the word pig?" (3)
- Guide the children to practice segmenting words using the Elkonian Boxes. For this activity the teacher prepares Elkonian Boxes ahead of time. Use card stack paper and draw two lines vertically on the paper. The card will have three areas. These areas are referred to as boxes. Each student will get a card and three plastic chips. When you say, for example, the word pig very slowly such as /p/-/p/-/p/-/p/, the children should push one chip into the first box; when you say /i/-/i/-/i/-/i/, they should push a chip into the second box; and when you say /g/-/g/-/g/, they should push a chip into the third box.

This exercise helps the children understand that the word pig is made up of three sounds. Continue with this activity using words with three sounds and some with two sounds until all the children are successful noting the different number of sounds in words.

As children gain experience with letter sounds use the Elkonian Boxes but this time instead of using chips to segment sounds in word, give them plastic alphabet letters to form words. Say a word and ask them to listen to the first sound in the word and to find the letter that represents that sound, continue with the medial sound and final sound of the word. Use words that have three sounds and some that have two sounds to help them become aware of the letters that represent sounds in words they know.

Evaluation (student behaviors to look for)
- Able to identify each sound in a word
- Able to blend and say the word
- Able to push the correct letter to each Elkonian Box to produce the correct word
- Use the Phoneme Segmentation Record Sheet by Hallie Kay Yopp (1995) to assess children's knowledge of sound segmentation
- Elkonian Cards
- Plastic alphabet lower case letters
- Tray to hold letters
- Dr. Seuss books that playfully reinforce the sounds in language
- Degan, B. *Jamberry* (New York: Harper and Row, 1983)

- Shaw, N. *Sheep on a Ship* (Boston: Houghton Mifflin, 1989)
- Most, B. *Cock-A-Doodle-Moo* (New York: Harcourt Brace, 1996)
- Leedy, L. *Pingo the Plaid Panda* (New York: Holiday House, 1989)
- Otto, C. *Dinosaur Chase* (New York Harper Trophy, 1991)
- Lesison, W. *Buzz Said the Bee* (New York Scholastic, 1992)

Use
- Whole Group
- Small Group
- Individual Student

TASK: SOUND MANIPULATION

Description
   The task of sound manipulation often referred to as "sound substitution" involves adding, or subtracting sound from words. In adding sounds to a rime the student forms a new word by manipulating the onset. For example, by adding f to ill the word fill is formed. By manipulating the onset f with w the new word becomes will. In the word win, if you subtract the w with another onset you form a new word.

Procedure
1. Engage students in manipulating the onset in the word win with other consonant sounds. For example, engage the students to substitute the onset with the following consonants: b, t, s, p to form the words bin, tin, sin, pin. You may also want to encourage students to add other consonants and form more words, even non-sense words such as l, d, n and form the non-sense words of lin, din, nin.
2. Read to students books with words that can be easily changed by manipulating beginning, middle or ending sounds. Dr. Seuss's books are excellent to develop sound manipulation. For example, Dr. Seuss's (1974), "There's a Wocket in My Pocket" reinforces sound manipulation throughout the tale.
3. Select words from the Phonogram list (Appendix F). For example begin with the short –a patterns: -am, -at, -an, continue with patterns in the order of difficulty and frequency. Begin with patterns most frequently occurring and easiest to learn patterns. Continue adding patterns as children develop mastery, for example, first begin with am, follow with the –at pattern, then the –an pattern.
4. Pattern words for the –am pattern are: am, ham, jam, Sam, Pam. Have students subtract the onset of each word until they recognize that the rime is the same for all words. Have students add the onset to form

the words. Continue with this activity so that students see the concept of onset and rime.

5. Have children whose names fit this pattern come to the front of the class: For example, Pam and Sam come to the front of the room. Ask the rest of the children to remove the onset (beginning sound) from Pam, and tell what is left? The students should say, "-am". Continue with Sam's name: S -am = SAM.

6. Shared reading: Read Dr. Seuss's (1988) "Green Eggs and Ham".

7. Bring to class a jar of jam and a can of ham labels. Have students point to the words that have the –am at the end of the word. Engage students in subtracting the j from –am and then putting it together: j—am = jam; h—am = ham.

8. Cookie-Sheet and magnetic letters: Using a cookie sheet and magnetic letters form words using phonograms or word patterns (see Appendix for list): -am with j, h. Have students take turns form word: jam, ham; subtract the beginning sound so that the word pattern is left –am. Have the students say the word as they manipulate the onset and rime.

Evaluation (student behaviors to look for)
- Able to identify onset
- Able to identify rime
- Able to blend onset and rime
- Accuracy of blending onset and rime

Materials/Resources
Cookie sheet
Magnetic letters
Dr. Seuss's (1988) "Green Eggs and Ham"

Use
- Whole Group
- Small Group
- Individual Student

TASK: SOUND ISOLATION

Description
The task of sound isolation is also referred as oddity tasks (Adams, 1991). Students in sound isolation or oddity tasks have to determine sounds in a word: (1) beginning sounds; (2) medial sounds; and (3) final sounds. An instructional technique to help students isolate sounds in words is presenting a series of words that begin with the same sound.

Students may be presented with a series of words that begin with the same sound, such as cat, cot, cup, cap and asked to tell the beginning sound of each word. Then the teacher can ask the students which sound they hear in the word "cat" and "cap", which sound in the word "cot" and which sound in the word "cup". For the final sound, the teacher may ask, "Which words end wi th the /t/?" "Which words end with /p/?" The same procedure can be used for determining word families and rimes.

Once the students have acquired proficiency with familiar words, the teacher can challenge them with sound isolation tasks with words that begin with different sounds. A series of words such as dog, pan, sit, mad can be presented and students are asked to analyze the individual sounds in the beginning, medial, and final position.

Procedure
1. Ask students to identify the beginning, middle, and ending sounds in words. For example, ask, "What is the beginning sound in rose?" "What is the ending sound in pig?" "What is the sound you hear in the middle of cat?"
2. Engage students in activities that help to isolate sounds in words. A song that teaches sound isolation is "Old MacDonald Had a Farm" (Yopp, 1992) (see Appendix B). In this song, students are asked to tell what sounds they hear at the beginning, middle or end of words.
3. You may use the same sound for each position (beginning, middle, and end) as you begin to work with a new sound and then mix them up as children learn more sounds.

   Ask the children, What's the sound that
      starts these words: turtle, time, and teeth?
   Wait for a response from the children—
      (/t/).
   Say, /t/ is the sound that starts these
      words: turtle, time and teeth.
   With a /t/, /t/, here and a /t/,/t/, there,
   Here a /t/, there a /t/, everywhere a
      /t/, /t/,/t/ is the sound that starts
      these words: turtle, time, and teeth.
   What is the sound in the middle of these
      words: beet and meal and read?
   Wait for a response from the children
      - /ee/.
   /ee/ is the sound in the middle of these
      words: beet and meal and read.
   With a /ee/, /ee/, here and a /ee/, /ee/,
      there,
   Here a /ee/, there a /ee/, everywhere a
      /ee/, /ee/.

/ee/ is the sound in the middle of these
  words: beet and meal and read.
What's the sound at the end of these
  words: bed and seed and mad?
Wait for a response from the children
  - /d/.
/d/ is the sound at the end of these
  words: bed and seed and mad.
With a /d/, /d/, here and a /d/, /d/, there,
Here a /d/, there a /d/, everywhere a
  /d/, /d/.
/d/ is the sound at the end of these words: bed and seed and mad.

4. Continue with this playful exercise in teaching children sound isolation. Also, teach the children to speak like a ghost as they isolate the
sounds in words they already know. Tell the children that you are going to speak like a ghost with some words they already know. They are
to tell you beginning, middle, and ending sounds in words:
/b/ /b/ /b/ /b/ /b/ /e/ /e/ /e/ /e/ /e/ /d/ /d/ /d/ /d/ /d/ = bed
/s//s//s//s//s//s/ /ee/ /ee/ /ee/ /ee/ /d/ /d/ /d/ /d/ /d/ = seed
Continue with the following word: meal, read, mad.

Evaluation (student behaviors to look for)
- Able to identify beginning sounds
- Able to identify middle sounds
- Able to identify ending sounds

Materials/Resources
  Song: Old MacDonald had a Farm (see Appendix B)
  Word Cards

Use
- Whole Group
- Small Group
- Individual Student

TASK: SOUND MATCHING

Description
  When a teacher asks students to think of words that begin with a specific
sound the task is referred to as sound matching. For example, the teacher
may say, what words or names begin with the sound /s/ makes. The students

may say words that they already know, such as, sat, soap, sand, say, Sandra. The teacher can extend this task and challenge the students to match medial sounds (vowel or vowel combinations), final sounds (rime, e.g., -at, -ip-ay- and . . .), rhyming words (make, take, cake . . .), and syllables. Challenge the students to discriminate beginning sounds among a series of words, such as, cat, can, ran, fan, and tell which words begin with the same sound. Extend the challenge to medial sounds, final sound, rhyming words and words with different number of syllables.

Procedure
1. Ask the students, "Do cookie and cup begin with the same sound?" Continue with pairs of words that begin with the same sound so that the children understand that they are listening for the sound that begins the word. Add words that do not begin with the same sound to see if the children can detect the difference in the word pair (cap–tap).
2. Ask the students, "Do cup and map ends with the same sound?" Continue with pairs of words that end with the same sound, then add word pairs that do not end with the same sound to see if the children can detect the difference in the word pair (cap–cat).
3. Play the matching game by asking children, "Which one does not belong: cat, rat, cookie. Which one does not belong: hat, fit, cap?

Evaluation (student behaviors to look for)
• Able to identify beginning sounds
• Able to identify ending sounds

Materials/Resources
Word Pairs matching beginning sounds
Word Pairs not matching beginning sounds
Word pairs matching ending sounds
Word pairs not matching ending sounds

Use
• Whole Group
• Small Group
• Individual Student

TASK: RHYMING AND ALLITERATION

Knowledge of nursery rhymes has been related to early reading skills (Adams, 1991; Maclean, Bryant, and Bradley, 1987) furthermore, these researchers found that early knowledge of nursery rhymes was strongly and specifically related to the development of more abstract phonological skills (e.g., knowledge of sounds, recognition of letters and words) and of emergent reading abilities.

Knowledge of rhyme and alliteration is a simpler task for many young children. This task requires little more than the detection of rhyme and alliteration. Rhyming words such as those heard in the Mother Goose verse for children, "Hey, diddle, diddle! The cat and the fiddle, The cow jumped over the moon, The little dog laughed to see such sport, And the dish ran away with spoon," are playful and interesting to young children. Invite them to join in and add the rhyming word or make up their own rhymes. Other favorites are, "Little Miss Muffet sat on a Tuffet", "Jack and Jill went up the Hill". Many verses rhyme at the end of each line, but some also use internal rhyming elements, such as those in "Hickory, dickory, doc, the mouse ran up the clock". Also very helpful is bringing nursery rhymes with the repetition of sounds in a phrase or line.

- After you read a poem or sing a song together, ask the children to find the rhyming words.
- Generate other words that rhyme with the rhyming words in today's shared reading.
- Read open-ended songs that lend themselves to having verses added such as:
    "My Aunt Came Back"
    "Down by the Bay"

Evaluation (student behaviors to look for)
- Able to hear rhyme in word pairs
- Able to hear rhyme in poems, songs, rhyming verses
- Able to build rhymes
- Accuracy of identifying rhymes

Materials/Resources
Word Cards with rhyming or non-rhyming word pairs
Rhyming verses (see Appendix for additional rhyming verses) such as:
Down by the bay, where the watermelons grow
Back to my home I dare not go
For if I do my mother will say,
Did you ever see a bear combing his hair down by the bay.
Did you ever see a bee with a sunburned knee down by the bay?
Did you ever see a moose kissing a goose down by the bay?
Did you ever see a whale with a polka-dot tail down by the bay?
Did you ever see a fish sailing in a dish down by the bay?

Did you ever see a cat in a tall black hat down by the bay?
What could a bee see sitting in a tree down by the bay?

Baa, Baa, Black Sheep
Baa, baa, black sheep,
Have you any wool?
Yes sir, yes sir,
Three bags full.

One for the master,
One for the dame,
But none for the little boy
Who cries in the lane.

Fuzzy, Wuzzy was a bear.
Fuzzy, Wuzzy had no hair.
Fuzzy Wuzzy wasn't fuzzy,
Was he?

Hiccup, hiccup, go away!
Come again another day.
Hiccup, hiccup, when I bake,
I'll give to you a butter-cake.

Use

- Whole Group
- Small Group
- Individual Student

PHONEMIC AWARENESS

Consonant Letter Instruction and Interactive-Multisensory Activities

The consonant letter instruction and interactive activities that follow began with the letter b and end with the letter z. The organization of the instruction begins with the high-frequency consonants and follows with the lower-frequency consonants and y. The high frequency consonants are referred to as continuants. Continuants are speech sounds produced by releasing a continuous stream of breath. They are easier to say and to detect in isolation. The sequence is based on the frequency with which the correspondences appear and their estimated level of difficulty. Special attention must be given to the s, l, r, when teaching the sounds they represent since some children up to age 5–6 have problems with these sounds (Beaty, 1994). The lower- frequency consonants and y follow. This organization follows Gunning (2000) sequencing of phonemic elements: high frequency consonants, lower-frequency consonants and y. The variations of the letters c, g, and x are included to provide a program of systematic instruction.

High-frequency consonants s, m, b, f, r, g, l, c /k/, n, h, t, d are developed in the following units of instruction.

PHONEMIC AWARENESS UNIT: s /s/

Goal: To introduce the s = /s/ correspondence.
Procedure:
Have students listen to the s = /s/ correspondence.
Have the students listen to the /s/ in the following words:

    Sam
    soup
    sand
    sat
    say

Blend onset and rime with the correspondence words:

(onset)	(rime)	
/s/	/at/ -	/sat/
/s/	/it/ -	/sit/
/s/	/et/ -	/set/
/s/	/am/ -	/Sam/
/s/	/and/ -	/sand/

Activities:
Introduce the rhyme: "A Sailor Went to Sea." Student repeat the rhyme with the teacher.

A sailor went to sea
To see what he could see
And all that he could see
Was the sea, sea, sea.
(For other rhymes see Appendix B)

Segmentation: Using a rubber band explain the concept of "stretch".
Teacher Models:
- Using a rubber band show how to stretch a word as the word is said: /sssssssssss/ - /aaaaaaa/ - /tttttttttttt/.
- Bring the rubber band back to its original length and says the word fast - /sat/.
- Students and teacher continue with this process with the rest of the /s/ words.

Segmentation and Blending

The teacher pronounces the sounds individually very slowly in a word and asks the students to say the word very fast. For example, tell the students, "I am going to say a word very slowly and then I will say it very fast". Listen: /s/ - /a / - /t/. That is the slow way. I am going to say the word very fast: /sat/. Now I am going to say another word very slowly: /s/ - /i/ - /t/. Can you say it fast? sit! Segmentation is the opposite of blending. Stretching the pronunciation of words helps the students hear the separate sounds in a word. The student is blending also in this process. After the students can blend the sounds, the teacher can begin to have the student segment the sounds, too. After students can segment sounds, engage them in blending and segmenting activities by having them say a word slow and then saying it fast.

Manipulate the sounds

Tell the students, "I can make a new word from sat by changing the /s/ to an /f/". Can you tell me what the new word is? fat.
Continue sound manipulation with other onsets added to the rime –at. Example: pat, mat, chat . . .

Read Aloud

Listening to the reading is a natural way for children to become familiar with how language works. After children have listened to a story, have them go back into the book and find words. Write the words on the board or a flip chart. Have the children look for the sounds they already know. The more children listen to stories the more they develop sound/letter/word relationship on their own when they read. Suggested book that supports phonetic elements for the consonant s: *My Great Aunt Arizona* by Gloria Houston (HarperCollins, 1992).

Class Alphabet Book

Begin a class alphabet book with the initial consonants. Start with the S sound.

Alphabet Book: S /s

Give students homework on Monday. Through a newsletter to parents let them know that their child(ren) will be studying the sound of s. Tell parents to help their child(ren) collect pictures that they will bring to school that begin with the s sound as they will use them during instruction and then they will paste pictures in their Alphabet Book.

PRACTICE AND REINFORCEMENT ACTIVITIES

(See Appendix A)

The activities found in Appendix A are recommended for each consonant. These activities are described and exemplified but can be adapted to meet the needs of your students.

PHONEMIC AWARENESS UNIT: m /m/

Goal: To introduce the m = /m/ correspondence.
Procedure:
Have students listen to the m = /m/ correspondence.
Have the students listen to the /m/ in the following words:

mat	mop
mitt	mom
met	man
moon	mouse

Blend onset and rime with the correspondence words:

(onset)	(rime)	
/m/	/at/ -	/mat/
/m/	/op/ -	/mop/
/m/	/it/ -	/mit/
/m/	/ad/ -	/mad/
/m/	/om/ -	/mom/
/m/	/et/ -	/met/
/m/	/an/ -	/man/

Activities:
Introduce the rhyme: "The Three Little Kittens". Students repeat the rhyme with the teacher.

Segmentation: Using a rubber band explain the concept of "stretch".

Teacher Models:
- Using a rubber band show how to stretch a word as the word is said: /mmmmmmmm/-/aaaaaaa/-/nnnnnnnn/.
- Bring the rubber band back to its original length and says the word fast—/man/.
- Students and teacher continue with this process with the rest of the /m/ words.

Segmentation and Blending
The teacher pronounces the sounds individually very slowly in a word and asks the students to say the word very fast. For example, tell the students, "I am going to say a word very slowly and then I will say it very fast". Listen: / m/ - /o / - /p/. That is the slow way. I am going to say the word very fast: /mop/. Now I am going to say another word very slowly: /m/ - /o/ - /m/. Can you say it fast? mom! Segmentation is the opposite of blending. Stretching the pronunciation of words helps the students hear the separate sounds in a word. The student is blending also in this process. After the

students can blend the sounds, the teacher can begin to have the student segment the sounds, too. After students can segment sounds, engage them in blending and segmenting activities by having them say a word slow and then saying it fast.

Manipulate the sounds
Tell the students, "I can make a new word from man by changing the /m/ to an /f/". Can you tell me what the new word is? fan.

Read Aloud
Listening to the reading is a natural way for children to become familiar with how language works. After children have listened to a story, have them go back into the book and find words. Write the words on the board or a flip chart. Have the children look for the sounds they already know. The more children listen to stories the more they develop sound/letter/word relationship on their own when they read. Suggested book that supports phonetic elements for the consonant m: *My Great Aunt Arizona* by Gloria Houston (HarperCollins, 1992).

Class Alphabet Book
Begin a class alphabet book with the initial consonants. The first letter and sound in the Class Alphabet Book is the Mm /m/.

Alphabet Book: Mm - /m/
Give students homework on Monday. Through a newsletter to parents let them know that their child(ren) will be studying the letter Mm all week. Tell parents to help their child(ren) collect pictures that they will bring to school that begin with the m /m/. Have students paste pictures that begin with the sound /m/ on the M page.

PRACTICE AND REINFORCEMENT ACTIVITIES

(See Appendix A)

The activities found in Appendix A are recommended for each consonant. These activities are described and exemplified but can be adapted to meet the needs of your students.

PHONEMIC AWARENESS UNIT

Goal: To develop the sound of B
Procedure:
  1. Have students listen to the sound of b in correspondence words:
     bat
     ball
     bee

bell
boat
book
baby

2. Have the students listen to the /b / in the following words with pictures again:

bat   ball   bee   book   bell   book   baby   bun   boat

Guide pupils to blend onset and rime with the correspondence words:

(onset)	(rime)	
/ b /	/ad/ -	/bad/
/ b/	/og/ -	/bog/
/b/	/ig/ -	/big/

Activities:

Introduce the rhyme, "Baa, Baa, Black Sheep." Students repeat the rhyme with the teacher.

Segmentation: Using a rubber band explain the concept of "stretch".

Teacher Models:
- Using a rubber band show how to stretch a word as the word is said: /bbbbb/ -/aaaaa-/dddddd/.
- Bring the rubber band back to its original length and says the word fast - /bad /.
- Students and teacher continue with this process with the rest of the words that began with the /b/.

Segmentation and Blending

The teacher tells the students, "We are going to play the game 'slow and fast'. The teacher pronounces the sounds individually very slowly in a word and asks the students to say the word very fast. For example, tell the students, "I am going to say a word very slowly and then I will say it very fast". Listen: /b / - / a/ - /d/. That is the slow way. I am going to say the word very fast: / bad /. Now I am going to say another word very slowly: / b/ - / i/ - / g /. Can you say it fast? big!

Explain to the students that segmentation is the opposite of blending. Say, "When segmenting words, we stretch the pronunciation of words help you hear the separate sounds in a word." After stretching a word tell the student to bring the sounds back very quickly. Explain that this is called blending the sound and bring them back to say the word fast. After the students can blend the sounds, the teacher can begin to have the student segment the sounds, too. After students can segment sounds, engage them in blending and segmenting activities by having them say a word very slowly and then saying it fast.

Manipulate the sounds/Substitution
Tell the students, "Listen as I make a new word from big by changing the /b/ to a /p/". Can you tell me what the new word is? pig.

Read Aloud
Listening to the reading is a natural way for children to become familiar with how language works. After children have listened to a story, have them go back into the book and find words. Write the words on the board or a flip chart. Have the children look for the sounds they already know. The more children listen to stories the more they develop sound/letter/word relationship on their own when they read.

Suggested book that supports phonetic elements for the consonant b and the sound of b:

Class Alphabet Book
Continue with the class alphabet book with the initial consonant sound introduced to the students. The letter and sound in the Class Alphabet Book is the b.

Alphabet Book: B (sound of the week)
Give students homework on Monday. Through a newsletter (see Appendix E) for copy of newsletter you may wish to use. The newsletter, in English and in Spanish, lets parents know that their child will be studying the sound of b all week. Tell parents to help their child collect pictures that they will bring to school that begin with the b sound. Have students paste pictures that begin with the sound b on the B page.

PRACTICE AND REINFORCEMENT ACTIVITIES

(See Appendix A)

The following activities are recommended for the b consonant but can be adapted to other consonants. These activities are described in Appendix A.

PHONEMIC AWARENESS UNIT: f /f/

Goal: To introduce the f = /f/ correspondence.
Procedure:
Have students listen to the f = /f/ correspondence.
Have the students listen to the /f/ in the following words:

fan
five
fall
fit
fox
fat
fish
four

Blend onset and rime with the correspondence words:

(onset)	(rime)	
/f/	/at/ -	/fat/
/f/	/all/ -	/fall/
/f/	/ox/ -	/fox/
/f/	/ish/ -	/fish/

Activities:

Introduce the rhyme: " Fuzzy Wuzzy". Students repeat the rhyme with the teacher.

Segmentation: Using a rubber band explain the concept of "stretch".
1. Teacher Models:
   • using a rubber band show how to stretch a word as the word is said: /ffffffff-/aaaaaaa/-tttttttt/.
   • bring the rubber band back to its original length and says the word fast - /fat/.
   • students and teacher continue with this process with the rest of the /f/ words.

Segmentation and Blending

The teacher pronounces the sounds individually very slowly in a word and asks the students to say the word very fast. For example, tell the students, "I am going to say a word very slowly and then I will say it very fast". Listen: /f/ - /o/ - /x/. That is the slow way. I am going to say the word very fast: /fox/. Now I am going to say another word very slowly: /f/ - /i/ - /sh/. Can you say it fast? fish! Segmentation is the opposite of blending. Stretching the pronunciation of words helps the students hear the separate sounds in a word. The student is blending also in this process. After the students can blend the sounds, the teacher can begin to have the student segment the sounds, too. After students can segment sounds, engage them in blending and segmenting activities by having them say a word slow and then saying it fast.

Manipulate the sounds

Tell the students, "I can make a new word from fat by changing the /f/ to an /m/".
Can you tell me what the new word is? mat.

Read Aloud

Listening to the reading is a natural way for children to become familiar with how language works. After children have listened to a story, have them go back into the book and find words. Write the words on the board or a flip chart. Have the children look for the sounds they already know. The more children listen to stories the more they develop sound/letter/word relationship on their own when they read. Suggested book that supports phonetic elements for the consonant f: *The Bee Tree* by Patricia Polacco (Philomel Books, 1993).

Class Alphabet Book

Add to the class alphabet book with the initial consonant f /f/.

Alphabet Book: Ff - /f/

Give students homework on Monday. Through a newsletter to parents let them know that their child(ren) will be studying the letter Ff all week. Tell parents to help their child(ren) collect pictures that they will bring to school that begin with the f /f/. Have students paste pictures that begin with the sound /f/ on the F page.

PRACTICE AND REINFORCEMENT ACTIVITIES

(See Appendix A)

The activities found in Appendix A are recommended for each consonant. These activities are described and exemplified but can be adapted to meet the needs of your students.

PHONEMIC AWARENESS UNIT: r /r/

Goal: To introduce the r = /r/ correspondence.
Procedure:
Have students listen to the r = /r/ correspondence.
Have the students listen to the /r/ in the following words:

ran	rabbit
rug	radio
rat	rain
rake	row

Blend onset and rime with the correspondence words:

(onset)	(rime)	
/r/	/at/ -	/rat/
/r/	/ow/ -	/row/

/r/	/ug/ -	/rug/
/r/	/ake/ -	/rake/
/r/	/ain/ -	/rain/

Activities:
Introduce the rhyme: "Rain, Rain, Go Away". Students repeat the rhyme with the teacher.

Segmentation: Using a rubber band explain the concept of "stretch".
Teacher Models:
- Using a rubber band show how to stretch a word as the word is said: /rrrrrrr/-/aaaaaaa/-/ttttttttt/.
- Bring the rubber band back to its original length and says the word fast - /rat/.
- Students and teacher continue with this process with the rest of the /r/ words.

Segmentation and Blending
The teacher pronounces the sounds individually very slowly in a word and asks the students to say the word very fast. For example, tell the students, "I am going to say a word very slowly and then I will say it very fast". Listen: /r/ - /ow/. That is the slow way. I am going to say the word very fast: /row/. Now I am going to say another word very slowly: /r/ - /a/ - /ke/. Can you say it fast? rake! Segmentation is the opposite of blending. Stretching the pronunciation of words helps the students hear the separate sounds in a word. The student is blending also in this process. After the students can blend the sounds, the teacher can begin to have the student segment the sounds, too. After students can segment sounds, engage them in blending and segmenting activities by having them say a word slow and then saying it fast.

Manipulate the sounds
Tell the students, "I can make a new word from rat by changing the /r/ to an /n/".
Can you tell me what the new word is? nat.

Read Aloud
Listening to the reading is a natural way for children to become familiar with how language works. After children have listened to a story, have them go back into the book and find words. Write the words on the board or a flip chart. Have the children look for the sounds they already know. The more children listen to stories the more they develop sound/letter/word relationship on their own when they read. Suggested book that supports phonetic elements for the consonant n: *The Car Washing Street* by Denise Lewis Patrick (Tambourine Books, 1993).

Class Alphabet Book
Begin a class alphabet book with the initial consonants. The first letter and sound in the Class Alphabet Book is the Rr /r/.

Alphabet Book: Rr - /r/
Give students homework on Monday. Through a newsletter to parents let them know that their child(ren) will be studying the letter Rr all week. Tell parents to help their child(ren) collect pictures that they will bring to school that begin with the r /r/. Have students paste pictures that begin with the sound /r/ on the R page.

PRACTICE AND REINFORCEMENT ACTIVITIES

(See Appendix A)

The activities found in Appendix A are recommended for each consonant. These activities are described and exemplified but can be adapted to meet the needs of your students.

PHONEMIC AWARENESS UNIT: g /g/

Goal: To develop the sound of g followed by the vowels: a, o, u
Procedure:
1. Have students listen to the g correspondence.
2. Have the students listen to the /g / in the following words:
   gum
   go
   game
   Guide pupils to blend onset and rime with the correspondence words:

(onset)	(rime)	
/ g /	/um/ -	gum
/ g/	/o/ -	go
/ g/	/ig/ -	gig
/g/	/ame/ -	game
/g/	/ate/ -	gate
/g/	/oat/ -	goat
/g/	/irl/ -	girl

Activities:
Rhyme: Introduce the rhymes, "Gobble, Goggle" and" A-Hunting We Will Go". Students repeat the rhymes with the teacher.

Segmentation: Using a rubber band explain the concept of "stretch".

Teacher Models:
- Using a rubber band show how to stretch a word as the word is said: /gggggg/ -/uuuuu-/mmmmm/.
- Bring the rubber band back to its original length and says the word fast - /gum/.
- Students and teacher continue with this process with the rest of the words that began with the /g/.

Segmentation and Blending:
The teacher tells the students, "We are going to play the game 'slow and fast'. The teacher pronounces the sounds individually very slowly in a word and asks the students to say the word very fast. For example, tell the students, "I am going to say a word very slowly and then I will say it very fast". Listen: / g/ - / o/ - /t/. That is the slow way. I am going to say the word very fast: / got /. Now I am going to say another word very slowly: / g / - / a / - / te/. Can you say it fast? gate!

Segmentation is the opposite of blending. Stretching the pronunciation of words helps the students hear the separate sounds in a word. The student is blending also in this process. After the students can blend the sounds, the teacher can begin to have the student segment the sounds, too. After students can segment sounds, engage them in blending and segmenting activities by having them say a word very slowly and then saying it fast.

Manipulate the sounds/Substitution
Tell the students, "Listen as I make a new word from gig by changing the /_g/ to an /b/". Can you tell me what the new word is? big.

Read Aloud
Listening to the reading is a natural way for children to become familiar with how language works. After children have listened to a story, have them go back into the book and find words. Write the words on the board or a flip chart. Have the children look for the sounds they already know. The more children listen to stories the more they develop sound/letter/word relationship on their own when they read. Suggested book that supports phonetic elements for the consonant g: *The Bee Tree*, by Patricia Polacco (Philomel Books, 1993).

Class Alphabet Book
Add to the class alphabet book the initial consonant g. The letter and sound in the Class Alphabet Book is the /g/.

Alphabet Book: G (followed by a, o, u sound of the week)
Give students homework on Monday. Through a newsletter to parents let them know that their child will be studying the sound of the sound of g followed by a, o, u all week. Tell parents to help their child collect pictures that they will bring to school that begin with the g (followed by a,o,u) sound. Have students paste pictures that begin with the sound g on the G page.

PRACTICE AND REINFORCEMENT ACTIVITIES

(See Appendix A)

The activities found in Appendix A are recommended for each consonant. These activities are described and exemplified but can be adapted to meet the needs of your students.

PHONEMIC AWARENESS UNIT: l /l/

Goal: To introduce the l = /l/ correspondence.
Procedure:
Have students listen to the l = /l/ correspondence.
Have the students listen to the /l/ in the following words:

lion	ladder
lamp	leopard
lamb	lock

Blend onset and rime with the correspondence words:

(onset)	(rime)	
/l/	/ion/ -	/lion/
/l/	/amp/ -	/lamp/
/l/	/amb/ -	/lamb/
/l/	/ock/ -	/lock/

Activities:
Introduce the rhyme: "Looby Loo". Students repeat the rhyme with the teacher.

Segmentation: Using a rubber band explain the concept of "stretch".

Teacher Models:
- Using a rubber band show how to stretch a word as the word is said: /llllllll/-/iiiiiiii/-/oooooooo-nnnnnnnn/.
- Bring the rubber band back to its original length and says the word fast - /lion/.
- Students and teacher continue with this process with the rest of the /l/ words.

Segmentation and Blending

The teacher pronounces the sounds individually very slowly in a word and asks the students to say the word very fast. For example, tell the students, "I am going to say a word very slowly and then I will say it very fast". Listen: /l/ - /a/ - /m/ - /p/. That is the slow way. I am going to say the word very fast: /lamp/. Now I am going to say another word very slowly: /l/ - /o/ - /c/ - /k/. Can you say it fast? lock! Segmentation is the opposite of blending. Stretching the pronunciation of words helps the students hear the separate sounds in a word. The student is blending also in this process. After the students can blend the sounds, the teacher can begin to have the student segment the sounds, too. After students can segment sounds, engage them in blending and segmenting activities by having them say a word slow and then saying it fast.

Manipulate the sounds

Tell the students, "I can make a new word from lock by changing the /l/ to an /r/". Can you tell me what the new word is? rock!

Read Aloud

Listening to the reading is a natural way for children to become familiar with how language works. After children have listened to a story, have them go back into the book and find words. Write the words on the board or a flip chart. Have the children look for the sounds they already know. The more children listen to stories the more they develop sound/letter/word relationship on their own when they read. Suggested book that supports phonetic elements for the consonant l: *My Great Aunt Arizona* by Gloria Houston (HarperCollins, 1992).

Class Alphabet Book

Begin a class alphabet book with the initial consonants. The first letter and sound in the Class Alphabet Book is the Ll /l/.

Alphabet Book: Ll - /l/

Give students homework on Monday. Through a newsletter to parents let them know that their child(ren) will be studying the letter Ll all week. Tell parents to help their child(ren) collect pictures that they will bring to school that begin with the l /l/. Have students paste pictures that begin with the sound /l/ on the L page.

PRACTICE AND REINFORCEMENT ACTIVITIES

(See Appendix A)

The activities found in Appendix A are recommended for each consonant. These activities are described and exemplified but can be adapted to meet the needs of your students.

PHONEMIC AWARENESS UNIT: c /k/

Goal: To introduce the sound c makes in initial position.
Procedure:
   Have students listen to the sound the c makes in words such as: cat, cot,
   cut.
   Have the students listen to the sound c makes in the following words:
      can
      cat
      corn
      comb
      cup
      cake
      car
      carrot

Rhyming and Matching Sounds
   Introduce students to the knowledge of phonemic awareness by reading
nursery rhymes.
   a. Read the nursery rhyme: "What Animals Say"
      Bow-wow, says the dog,
      Mew, mew, says the cat,
      Grunt, grunt, goes the hog,
      And squeak goes the rat.
      Tu-whoo, says the owl,
      Caw, caw, says the crow,
      Quack, quack, says the duck,
      What cuckoos say you know.
   Ask students which words rhyme.
   Ask students to match the ending sounds of words:
            say   day   may   pay   lay
            Ask students to identify the ending sound (/ay/) of the words.
   Introduce the concept of blending with onsets and rimes. Tell the students to blend the parts of the following words:
   Blend onset and rime with the correspondence words:
         (onset)   (rime)
Explain and demonstrate the blending one-syllable word; onset and rime
in the following words:
   c   at   cat
   c   an   /can/
   c   up   /cup/
   c   orn   corn

Segmentation:
> Because segmentation is a difficult task for most young children, the teacher models with a familiar word. The teacher segments the word "man" by telling the students that she/he is going to stretch the word "man" as follows:

> mmmmmm aaaaa nnnnn - man

Have students help you put the word back: /man/

Activity
> Using a rubber band explain the concept of "stretch". Tell the students that they are going to "stretch" the sounds in words and then they are going to quickly bring the sounds together to say the word.

Teacher Models:
- using a rubber band demonstrate how to stretch a word as the word is said: cccccc-/uuuuuuuu/-pppppppp/.
- bring the rubber band back to its original size and say the word fast—"cup".
- students and teacher continue with this process with the rest of the words that begin with the letter c.

Segmentation and Blending
> The teacher pronounces the sounds individually very slowly in a word and asks the students to say the word very fast. For example, tell the students, "I am going to say a word very slowly and then I will say it very fast". Listen: /c/ - /u/ - /p/. That is the slow way. I am going to say the word very fast: /cup/. Now I am going to say another word very slowly: /c/ - /a/ - /n/. Can you say it fast? can! Segmentation is the opposite of blending. Stretching the pronunciation of words helps the students hear the separate sounds in a word. The student is blending also in this process. After the students can blend the sounds, the teacher can begin to have the student segment the sounds, too. After students can segment sounds, engage them in blending and segmenting activities by having them say a word slow and then saying it fast.

Manipulate the sounds
> Tell the students, "I can make a new word from cat by changing the /c/ to an /f/".
> Can you tell me what the new word is? fat.
> Follow the activity by substituting with the following onsets: p, m, r, n.

Read Aloud
> Listening to the reading is a natural way for children to become familiar with how language works. After children have listened to a story, have them

go back into the book and find words. Write the words on the board or a flip chart. Have the children look for the sounds they already know. The more children listen to stories the more they develop sound/letter/word relationship on their own when they read. Suggested book that supports phonetic elements for the consonant c /k/: *Dragonfly's Tale* by Kristina Rodana (Clarion, 1991).

Alphabet Book

Continue adding to the alphabet book with the initial consonants. The letter and sound in the Class Alphabet Book is the Cc /k/.

Alphabet Book: Cc - /k/

Ownership is important to young children. Begin phonemic awareness instruction by letting parents know that their child will be studying sounds throughout the school year. One form of homework is to help their child collect pictures that they will bring to school. Inform the parents that each Monday the class will be studying a letter. The child is to collect pictures that begin with the letter of the week. For the current unit the children are studying the letter c.

Tell the parents to help their child(ren) collect pictures that they will bring to school that begin with the letter c /k/. At the end of the instructional activities with the letter c Have students paste pictures that begin with the sound /k/ on the C page.

PRACTICE AND REINFORCEMENT ACTIVITIES

The following activities are recommended for each consonant. These activities are described and exemplified in Appendix A.

Syllable Clap

I am thinking of an animal that begins with the /kkkkkk/ and it ends with at (cat).

Syllable Count

Engage children in a series of activities that help them realize that words are made up of syllables. Demonstrate by clapping to the syllables or word parts in the word: foosball.

Explain to children that knowing about syllables can help them when they read and write. Engage children in Syllable Clap. Ask them to clap with you as you say the following words:

sunshine	vacation	delicious	dinner
alphabet	calendar	school	wonderful

Rhyming Riddles using Onset and Rime-tricky rhyming riddles:

Ask children riddles that require them to manipulate sounds in their heads. Begin with ones that ask for endings, followed by ones that ask for a single consonant substitution at the beginning and ending with the most difficult ones that ask for a consonant blend or digraph at the beginning.

What rhymes with a cat and starts with /m/? mat
What rhymes with book and starts with /c/? cook
What rhymes with sing and starts with /r/? ring
What rhymes with log and starts with /f/? frog

Songs That Teach Sound Substitution:
Choose a song the students know and substitute a consonant sound for the beginning of each word in the song. A song (Yopp, 1992), that works well is from "I've Been Working on the Railroad":

Bee-Fi-Fibble-ee-I-Oh
Bee-Bi-biddle-ee-I-Oh
Dee-Di-Dibble-ee-I-Oh
Hee-Hi-Hiddle-ee-I-Oh

Stretchy Names and Stretchy Words-
Teacher and children clap and say a verse for each child in the class: Maggie, Maggie, how do you do? Who's that friend right next to you? Teacher and children say the next child's name very slowly, stretching palms far apart as the word is stretched: RRRRR-iiiii-ddddd-erererer.
Clap once quickly and say the name fast: "Ryder".
Alliteration Station: the teacher says a tongue twister and the children repeat it.

PHONEMIC AWARENESS UNIT: n /n/

Goal: To introduce the n = /n/ correspondence.
Procedure:
Have students listen to the n = /n/ correspondence.
Have the students listen to the /n/ in the following words:

net	nickle
nail	north
nine	neck
name	number
nat	

Blend onset and rime with the correspondence words:

(onset)	(rime)	
/n/	/et/ -	/net/
/n/	/at/ -	/nat/
/n/	/ame/ -	/name/

Activities:
  Introduce the rhyme: "Engine, Engine, Number Nine". Students repeat
  the rhyme with the teacher.

Segmentation: Using a rubber band explain the concept of "stretch".

Teacher Models:
  • Using a rubber band show how to stretch a word as the word is
    said: /nnnnnnnn/-/eeeeeeee/-/tttttttt/.
  • Bring the rubber band back to its original length and says the word
    fast - /net/.
  • Students and teacher continue with this process with the rest of the
    /n/ words.

Segmentation and Blending
  The teacher pronounces the sounds individually very slowly in a word
  and asks the students to say the word very fast. For example, tell the students, "I am going to say a word very slowly and then I will say it very
  fast". Listen: /n/ - /a/ - /t/. That is the slow way. I am going to say the word
  very fast: /nat/. Now I am going to say another word very slowly: /n/ - /i/
  - /n/ - (silent /e/). Can you say it fast? nine! Segmentation is the opposite
  of blending. Stretching the pronunciation of words helps the students
  hear the separate sounds in a word. The student is blending also in this
  process. After the students can blend the sounds, the teacher can begin to
  have the student segment the sounds, too. After students can segment
  sounds, engage them in blending and segmenting activities by having
  them say a word slow and then saying it fast.

Manipulate the sounds
  Tell the students, "I can make a new word from net by changing the /n/
  to a /p/". Can you tell me what the new word is? pet.

Read Aloud
  Listening to the reading is a natural way for children to become familiar with how language works. After children have listened to a story,
  have them go back into the book and find words. Write the words on
  the board or a flip chart. Have the children look for the sounds they
  already know. The more children listen to stories the more they develop sound/letter/word relationship on their own when they read.
  Suggested book that supports phonetic elements for the consonant n:
  The Car Washing Street by Denise Lewis Patrick (Tambourine Books,
  1993).

Class Alphabet Book
  Begin a class alphabet book with the initial consonants. The first letter
  and sound in the Class Alphabet Book is the Nn /n/.

Alphabet Book: Nn - /n/

Give students homework on Monday. Through a newsletter to parents let them know that their child(ren) will be studying the letter Nn all week. Tell parents to help their child(ren) collect pictures that they will bring to school that begin with the n /n/. Have students paste pictures that begin with the sound /n/ on the N page.

PRACTICE AND REINFORCEMENT ACTIVITIES

(See Appendix A)

The activities found in Appendix A are recommended for each consonant. These activities are described and exemplified but can be adapted to meet the needs of your students.

PHONEMIC AWARENESS UNIT: h /h/

Goal: To develop the sound of h
Procedure:

Have students listen to the /h/ correspondence.

Have the students listen to the /h / in the following words:

hat
ham
hog
hand
hook
horn
horse
house

Guide pupils to blend onset and rime with the correspondence words:

(onset)	(rime)	
/ h /	/at/ -	hat
/h /	/og/ -	hog
/h /	/ug/ -	hug
/h/	/am/ -	ham
/h/	/and/ -	hand
/h/	/ook/ -	hook
/h/	/orn/ -	horn

Activities:

Rhyme: Introduce the rhyme, "Hiccup, Hiccup". Students repeat the rhyme with the teacher.

Segmentation: Using a rubber band explain the concept of "stretch".

Teacher Models:
- Using a rubber band show how to stretch a word as the word is said: /hhhhh/ -/aaaaa-/tttttt/.
- Bring the rubber band back to its original length and says the word fast - /hat /.
- Students and teacher continue with this process with the rest of the words that began with the /h/.

Segmentation and Blending:
The teacher tells the students, "we are going to play the game 'slow and fast'."

The teacher pronounces the sounds individually very slowly in a word and asks the students to say the word very fast. For example, tell the students, "I am going to say a word very slowly and then I will say it very fast". Listen: / h/ - / o/ - /g/. That is the slow way. I am going to say the word very fast: /hog /. Now I am going to say another word very slowly: / h / - / a / - / m /. Can you say it fast? ham!

Segmentation is the opposite of blending. Stretching the pronunciation of words helps the students hear the separate sounds in a word. The student is blending also in this process. After the students can blend the sounds, the teacher can begin to have the student segment the sounds, too. After students can segment sounds, engage them in blending and segmenting activities by having them say a word very slowly and then saying it fast.

Manipulate the sounds/Substitution
Tell the students, "Listen as I make a new word from og by changing the /h/ to an /l/". Can you tell me what the new word is? log.

Read Aloud
Listening to the reading is a natural way for children to become familiar with how language works. After children have listened to a story, have them go back into the book and find words. Write the words on the board or a flip chart. Have the children look for the sounds they already know. The more children listen to stories the more they develop sound/letter/word relationship on their own when they read.

Class Alphabet Book
Begin a class alphabet book with the initial consonant sound introduced to the students. The letter and sound in the Class Alphabet Book is the h /h/.

Alphabet Book: h (sound of the week)

Give students homework on Monday. Through a newsletter to parents let them know that their child will be studying the sound of h all week. Tell parents to help their child collect pictures that they will bring to school that begin with the h sound. Have students paste pictures that begin with the sound h on the h page.

PRACTICE AND REINFORCEMENT ACTIVITIES

(See Appendix A)

The activities found in Appendix A are recommended for each consonant. These activities are described and exemplified but can be adapted to meet the needs of your students.

PHONEMIC AWARENESS UNIT: t /t/

Goal: To develop the sound of t
Procedure:
Have students listen to the /t/ correspondence.
Have the students listen to the /t / in the following words:
tan
top
ten
tip
tire
toe
tiger
table
tent
teeth
Guide pupils to blend onset and rime with the correspondence words:

(onset)	(rime)	
/ t/	/an -	tan
/ t/	/oe/ -	toe
/ t/	/op/ -	top

Activities:

Rhyme: Introduce the rhyme, "Little Tommy Tucker". Have the students repeat the rhyme with the teacher.

Segmentation: Using a rubber band explain the concept of "stretch".
Teacher Models:
- Using a rubber band show how to stretch a word as the word is said: /ttttttt/- /eeeeee/ -/nnnnnn/.
- Bring the rubber band back to its original length and says the word fast - /ten /.
- Students and teacher continue with this process with the rest of the words that began with the /t/.

Segmentation and Blending

The teacher tells the students, "We are going to play the game 'slow and fast'." The teacher pronounces the sounds individually very slowly in a word and asks the students to say the word very fast. For example, tell the students, "I am going to say a word very slowly and then I will say it very fast". Listen: / t/ - /o / - /p/. That is the slow way. I am going to say the word very fast: / top /. Now I am going to say another word very slowly: / t / - /i / - / p /. Can you say it fast? tip!

Segmentation is the opposite of blending. Stretching the pronunciation of words helps the students hear the separate sounds in a word. The student is blending also in this process. After the students can blend the sounds, the teacher can begin to have the student segment the sounds, too. After students can segment sounds, engage them in blending and segmenting activities by having them say a word very slowly and then saying it fast.

Manipulate the sounds/Substitution

Tell the students, "Listen as I make a new word from op by changing the /t/ in /top/ to a /p/". Can you tell me what the new word is? pop.

Read Aloud

Listening to the reading is a natural way for children to become familiar with how language works. After children have listened to a story, have them go back into the book and find words. Write the words on the board or a flip chart. Have the children look for the sounds they already know. The more children listen to stories the more they develop sound/letter/word relationship on their own when they read.

Class Alphabet Book

Begin a class alphabet book with the initial consonant sound introduced to the students. The letter and sound in the Class Alphabet Book is the t.

Alphabet Book: T (sound of the week)

Give students homework on Monday. Through a newsletter to parents let them know that their child will be studying the sound of the sound of T all week. Tell parents to help their child collect pictures that they will bring to school that begin with the T sound. Have students paste pictures that begin with the sound /t/ on the T page. After students complete the task, have them volunteer to say the names of the pictures.

PRACTICE AND REINFORCEMENT ACTIVITIES

(See Appendix A)

The activities found in Appendix A are recommended for each consonant. These activities are described and exemplified but can be adapted to meet the needs of your students.

PHONEMIC AWARENESS UNIT: d /d/

Goal: To develop the sound of d /d/.

Procedure:

Have students listen to the d = /d/ correspondence.

Have the students listen to the /d/ in the following words:

dad
desk
dog
dish
doll
deer
dig
door

Guide students to blend onset and rime with the correspondence words:

(onset)	(rime)	
/d/	/ad/ -	/dad/
/d/	/og/ -	/dog/
/d/	/ig/ -	/dig/

Activities:

Rhyme: Introduce the rhyme, "My Son John". Students repeat the rhyme with the teacher.

Segmentation: Using a rubber band explain the concept of "stretch".

Teacher Models:
- Using a rubber band show how to stretch a word as the word is said: /ddddddd-/aaaaa-/dddddd/.
- Bring the rubber band back to its original length and says the word fast - /dad/.
- Students and teacher continue with this process with the rest of the words that began with the /d/.

Segmentation and Blending
The teacher pronounces the sounds individually very slowly in a word and asks the students to say the word very fast. For example, tell the students, "I am going to say a word very slowly and then I will say it very fast". Listen: /d/ - /i/ - /g/. That is the slow way. I am going to say the word very fast: /dig/. Now I am going to say another word very slowly: /d/ - /o/-/l/. Can you say it fast? doll!

Segmentation is the opposite of blending. Stretching the pronunciation of words helps the students hear the separate sounds in a word. The student is blending also in this process. After the students can blend the sounds, the teacher can begin to have the student segment the sounds, too. After students can segment sounds, engage them in blending and segmenting activities by having them say a word very slowly and then saying it fast.

Manipulate the sounds/Substitution
Tell the students, " Listen as I make a new word from dig by changing the /d/ to a /p/". Can you tell me what the new word is? pig!

Read Aloud
Listening to the reading is a natural way for children to become familiar with how language works. After children have listened to a story, have them go back into the book and find words. Write the words on the board or a flip chart. Have the children look for the sounds they already know. The more children listen to stories the more they develop sound/letter/word relationship on their own when they read Suggested book that supports phonetic elements for the consonant d and the sound of d: *Ming Lo Moves the Mountain* by Arnold Lobel (Greenwillow, 1982).

Class Alphabet Book
Add to the class alphabet book the initial consonant sound introduced to the pupils. The first letter and sound in the Class Alphabet Book is the Dd /d/.

Alphabet Book: Dd - /d/

Give students homework on Monday. Through a newsletter to parents let them know that their child will be studying the sound of the letter d all week. Tell parents to help their child collect pictures that they will bring to school that begin with the d sound. Have students paste pictures that begin with the sound /d/ on the D page.

PRACTICE AND REINFORCEMENT ACTIVITIES

The following activities are recommended for each consonant. These activities are described and exemplified in Appendix A.

Lower-frequency consonants and y

Lower-frequency consonants and y are: j, p, w, k, y, c /s/, g /j/, v, z, qu /kw/, x /ks/, x /z/. The units that follow develop these consonants and their sounds.

PHONEMIC AWARENESS UNIT

Goal: To introduce the j = /j/ correspondence.
Procedure:
Have students listen to the j = /j/ correspondence.
Have the students listen to the /j/ in the following words:

jar	jet
Jay	jeep
jeans	Jim (boy's name)
Jan (girl' name)	jig

Blend onset and rime with the correspondence words:

(onset)	(rime)	
/j/	/ar/ -	/jar/
/j/	/et/ -	/jet/
/j/	/am/ -	/jam/
/j/	/ig/ -	/jig/
/j/	/ay/ -	/jay/

Activities:
Introduce the rhyme: " Jack Be Nimble". Students repeat the rhyme with the teacher.

Segmentation: Using a rubber band explain the concept of "stretch".

Teacher Models:
- Using a rubber band show how to stretch a word as the word is said: /jjjjjjjj-/aaaaaaa/-rrrrrrrr/.
- Bring the rubber band back to its original length and says the word fast - /jar/.
- Students and teacher continue with this process with the rest of the /j/ words.

Segmentation and Blending

The teacher pronounces the sounds individually very slowly in a word and asks the students to say the word very fast. For example, tell the students, "I am going to say a word very slowly and then I will say it very fast". Listen: /j/ - /i / - /g/. That is the slow way. I am going to say the word very fast: /jig/. Now I am going to say another word very slowly: /j/ - /a/ - /m/. Can you say it fast? jam! Segmentation is the opposite of blending. Stretching the pronunciation of words helps the students hear the separate sounds in a word. The student is blending also in this process. After the students can blend the sounds, the teacher can begin to have the student segment the sounds, too. After students can segment sounds, engage them in blending and segmenting activities by having them say a word slow and then saying it fast.

Manipulate the sounds

Tell the students, "I can make a new word from jig by changing the /j/ to a /p/". Can you tell me what the new word is? pig.

Read Aloud

Listening to the reading is a natural way for children to become familiar with how language works. After children have listened to a story, have them go back into the book and find words. Write the words on the board or a flip chart. Have the children look for the sounds they already know. The more children listen to stories the more they develop sound/letter/word relationship on their own when they read. Suggested book that supports phonetic elements for the consonant j: *Too the Zoo: Animal Poems* selected by Lee Bennett Hopkins (Little, Brown, 1992).

Class Alphabet Book

Begin a class alphabet book with the initial consonants. The first letter and sound in the Class Alphabet Book is the Jj /j/.

Alphabet Book: Jj - /j/

Give students homework on Monday. Through a newsletter to parents let them know that their child(ren) will be studying the letter Jj all week. Tell parents to help their child(ren) collect pictures that they will bring to school that begin with the j /j/. Have students paste pictures that begin with the sound /j/ on the J page.

PRACTICE AND REINFORCEMENT ACTIVITIES

(See Appendix A)

The activities found in Appendix A are recommended for each consonant. These activities are described and exemplified but can be adapted to
meet the needs of your students.

Lower-frequency consonants and y are included in the instructional units
that follow. The consonants are: j, p, w, k, y, c/s/, g/j/, v, z, qu/kw/, x/ks/,x/z/.

PHONEMIC AWARENESS UNIT

Goal: To introduce the p = /p/ correspondence.
Procedure:
  Have students listen to the p = /p/ correspondence.
  Have the students listen to the /p/ in the following words:

pet	pen
pit	pie
pencil	pillow
purse	pup

Blend onset and rime with the correspondence words:

(onset)	(rime)	
/p/	/et/ -	/pet/
/p/	/en/ -	/pen/
/p/	/it/ -	/pit/
/p/	/up/ -	/pup/

Activities:
  Introduce the rhyme: "Pease Porridge". Students repeat the rhyme with
  the teacher.

Segmentation: Using a rubber band explain the concept of "stretch".

Teacher Models:
- Using a rubber band show how to stretch a word as the word is
said: /pppppppp/-/eeeeeeee/-/tttttttt/.
- Bring the rubber band back to its original length and says the word
fast - /pet/.
- Students and teacher continue with this process with the rest of the
/p/ words.

Segmentation and Blending
  The teacher pronounces the sounds individually very slowly in a word and
  asks the students to say the word very fast. For example, tell the students,

"I am going to say a word very slowly and then I will say it very fast". Listen: /p/ - /e / - /n/. That is the slow way. I am going to say the word very fast: /pen/. Now I am going to say another word very slowly: /p/ - /i/ - /t/. Can you say it fast? pit! Segmentation is the opposite of blending. Stretching the pronunciation of words helps the students hear the separate sounds in a word. The student is blending also in this process. After the students can blend the sounds, the teacher can begin to have the student segment the sounds, too. After students can segment sounds, engage them in blending and segmenting activities by having them say a word slow and then saying it fast.

Manipulate the sounds

Tell the students, "I can make a new word from pit by changing the /p/ to a /k/". Can you tell me what the new word is? kit.

Read Aloud

Listening to the reading is a natural way for children to become familiar with how language works. After children have listened to a story, have them go back into the book and find words. Write the words on the board or a flip chart. Have the children look for the sounds they already know. The more children listen to stories the more they develop sound/letter/word relationship on their own when they read. Suggested book that supports phonetic elements for the consonant p: *Sophie and Sammy's Library Sleepover* by Judith Caseley (Greenwillow, 1993).

Class Alphabet Book

Begin a class alphabet book with the initial consonants. The first letter and sound in the Class Alphabet Book is the Pp /p/.

Alphabet Book: Pp - /p/

Give students homework on Monday. Through a newsletter to parents let them know that their child(ren) will be studying the letter Pp all week. Tell parents to help their child(ren) collect pictures that they will bring to school that begin with the p /p/. Have students paste pictures that begin with the sound /p/ on the P page.

PRACTICE AND REINFORCEMENT ACTIVITIES

(See Appendix A)

The activities found in Appendix A are recommended for each consonant. These activities are described and exemplified but can be adapted to meet the needs of your students.

PHONEMIC AWARENESS UNIT

Goal: To introduce the w = /w/ correspondence.

Procedure:

Have students listen to the w = /w/ correspondence.

Have the students listen to the /w/ in the following words:

wig	well
wet	wagon
window	walk
web	weed

Blend onset and rime with the correspondence words:

(onset)	(rime)	
/w/	/et/ -	/wet/
/w/	/ig/ -	/wig/
/w/	/eb/ -	/web/
/w/	/ell/ -	/well/

Activities:

Introduce the rhyme: "Fuzzy Wuzzy". Students repeat the rhyme with the teacher.

> Fuzzy Wuzzy was a bear
> Fuzzy Wuzzy had no hair
> Fuzzy Wuzzy wasn't fuzzy,
> Was he?

Segmentation: Using a rubber band explain the concept of "stretch".

Teacher Models:

- Using a rubber band show how to stretch a word as the word is said: /wwwwwwww/-/eeeeeeee/-/tttttttt/.
- Bring the rubber band back to its original length and says the word fast - /wet/.
- Students and teacher continue with this process with the rest of the /w/ words.

Segmentation and Blending

The teacher pronounces the sounds individually very slowly in a word and asks the students to say the word very fast. For example, tell the students, "I am going to say a word very slowly and then I will say it very fast". Listen: /p/ - /e/ - /n/. That is the slow way. I am going to say the word very fast: /pen/. Now I am going to say another word very slowly: /w/ - /i/ - /g/. Can you say it fast? wig! Segmentation is the opposite of blending. Stretching the pronunciation of words helps the students hear the separate sounds in a word. The student is blending also in this process. After the students can blend the sounds, the teacher can begin to have the student segment the sounds, too. After students can segment sounds, engage them in blending and segmenting activities by having them say a word slow and then saying it fast.

Manipulate the sounds
Tell the students, "I can make a new word from wig by changing the /w/ to a /p/". Can you tell me what the new word is? pig.

Read Aloud
Listening to the reading is a natural way for children to become familiar with how language works. After children have listened to a story, have them go back into the book and find words. Write the words on the board or a flip chart. Have the children look for the sounds they already know. The more children listen to stories the more they develop sound/letter/word relationship on their own when they read. Suggested book that supports phonetic elements for the consonant w: *Sophie and Sammy's Library Sleepover* by Judith Caseley (Greenwillow, 1993).

Class Alphabet Book
Begin a class alphabet book with the initial consonants. The first letter and sound in the Class Alphabet Book is the Ww /w/.

Alphabet Book: Ww - /w/
Give students homework on Monday. Through a newsletter to parents let them know that their child(ren) will be learning the sound of the letter Ww all week. Tell parents to help their child(ren) collect pictures that they will bring to school that begin with the w /w/. Have students paste pictures that begin with the sound /w/ on the W page.

PRACTICE AND REINFORCEMENT ACTIVITIES

(See Appendix A)

The activities found in Appendix A are recommended for each consonant. These activities are described and exemplified but can be adapted to meet the needs of your students.

PHONEMIC AWARENESS UNIT

Goal: To introduce the k = /k/ correspondence.
Procedure:
Have students listen to the k = /k/ correspondence.

Have the students listen to the /k/ in the following picture card words:
key
kitten
kite
king
kettle
kangaroo

Blend onset and rime with the correspondence words:

(onset)	(rime)	
/k/	/ey/ -	/key/
/k/	/it/ -	/kit/
/k/	/ing/ -	/king/
/k/	/ite/ -	/kite/

Activities:
Introduce the rhyme: "Polly, Put the Kettle On". Students repeat the rhyme with the teacher.

Segmentation: Using a rubber band explainthe concept of "stretch".

Teacher Models:
- Using a rubber band show how to stretch a word as the word is said: /kkkkkkkk/-/iiiiiiii/-/tttttttt/.
- Bring the rubber band back to its original length and says the word fast - /kit/.
- Students and teacher continue with this process with the rest of the /k/ words.

Segmentation and Blending
The teacher pronounces the sounds individually very slowly in a word and asks the students to say the word very fast. For example, tell the students, "I am going to say a word very slowly and then I will say it very fast". Listen: /k/ - /i / - /t/ - /e/. That is the slow way. I am going to say the word very fast: /kit/. Now I am going to say another word very slowly: /k/ - /i/ - /n/ - /g/. Can you say it fast? king! Segmentation is the opposite of blending. Stretching the pronunciation of words helps the students hear the separate sounds in a word. The student is blending also in this process. After the students can blend the sounds, the teacher can begin to have the student segment the sounds, too. After students can segment sounds, engage them in blending and segmenting activities by having them say a word slow and then saying it fast.

Manipulate the sounds
Tell the students, "I can make a new word from kit by changing the /k/ to a /p/". Can you tell me what the new word is? pit.

Read Aloud

    Listening to the reading is a natural way for children to become familiar with how language works. After children have listened to a story, have them go back into the book and find words. Write the words on the board or a flip chart. Have the children look for the sounds they already know. The more children listen to stories the more they develop sound/letter/word relationship on their own when they read. Suggested book that supports phonetic elements for the consonant k: *Ming Lo Moves the Mountain* by Arnold Lobel (Greenwillow, 1982).

Class Alphabet Book

    Begin a class alphabet book with the initial consonants. The first letter and sound in the Class Alphabet Book is the Kk /k/.

Alphabet Book: Kk - /k/

    Give students homework on Monday. Through a newsletter to parents let them know that their child(ren) will be studying the letter Kk all week. Tell parents to help their child(ren) collect pictures that they will bring to school that begin with the k /k/. Have students paste pictures that begin with the sound /k/ on the K page.

PRACTICE AND REINFORCEMENT ACTIVITIES

(See Appendix A)

    The activities found in Appendix A are recommended for each conso-nant. These activities are described and exemplified but can be adapted to meet the needs of your students.

PHONEMIC AWARENESS UNIT

Goal: To introduce the y = /y/ correspondence.
Procedure:
    Have students listen to the y = /y/ correspondence.
    Have the students listen to the /y/ in the following words:

yak	yawn	yucca
yarn	yoke	yo-yo
yogurt	yellow	

Blend onset and rime with the correspondence words:

(onset)	(rime)	
/y/	/ak/ -	/yak/
/y/	/arn/ -	/yarn/
/y/	/awn/-	/yawn/

Activities:
Introduce the rhyme: "Clouds" by Christine Rossetti. Students repeat the rhyme with the teacher.

> White sheep, white sheep,
> On a blue hill,
> When the wind stops
> You all stand still.
>
> When the wind blows
> You walk away slow,
> White sheep, white sheep,
> Where do you go?

Segmentation: Using a rubber band explain the concept of "stretch".

Teacher Models:
- Using a rubber band show how to stretch a word as the word is said: /yyyyyyyy/-/aaaaaaa /-/kkkkkkk/.
- Bring the rubber band back to its original length and says the word fast - /yak/.
- Students and teacher continue with this process with the rest of the /y/ words.

Segmentation and Blending
The teacher pronounces the sounds individually very slowly in a word and asks the students to say the word very fast. For example, tell the students, "I am going to say a word very slowly and then I will say it very fast". Listen: /y/ - /ar/ - /n/. That is the slow way. I am going to say the word very fast: /yarn/. Now I am going to say another word very slowly: /y/ - /aw/ - /n/. Can you say it fast? yawn! Segmentation is the opposite of blending. Stretching the pronunciation of words helps the students hear the separate sounds in a word. The student is blending also in this process. After the students can blend the sounds, the teacher can begin to have the student segment the sounds, too. After students can segment sounds, engage them in blending and segmenting activities by having them say a word slowly and then saying it fast (/y/ /y/ /y/ y/y /e/ /e/ /e/ /e/ /l/ /l/ /l/ = yell). Add more words that begin with the /y/ sound.

Manipulate the sounds
Tell the students, "I can make a new word from yell by changing the /y/ to an /f/". Can you tell me what the new word is? fell.
Change the /f/ to /t/ and the new words is ? tell
Continue adding beginning sounds even if it makes a non-sense word.

Read Aloud

Listening to the reading is a natural way for children to become familiar with how language works. After children have listened to a story, have them go back into the book and find words. Write the words on the board or a flip chart. Have the children look for the sounds they already know. The more children listen to stories the more they develop sound/letter/word relationship on their own when they read. Suggested book that supports phonetic elements for the consonant y: *Dragonfly's Tale* by Kristina Rodanas, (Clarion, 1991).

Class Alphabet Book

Begin a class alphabet book with the initial consonants. The first letter and sound in the Class Alphabet Book is the Yy /y/.

Alphabet Book: Yy - /y/

Give students homework on Monday. Through a newsletter to parents let them know that their child(ren) will be learning the sound the letter Yy makes all week. Tell parents to help their child(ren) collect pictures that they will bring to school that begin with the y /y/. Have students paste pictures that begin with the sound /y/ on the Y page.

PRACTICE AND REINFORCEMENT ACTIVITIES

(See Appendix A)

The activities found in Appendix A are recommended for each consonant. These activities are described and exemplified but can be adapted to meet the needs of your students.

PHONEMIC AWARENESS UNIT

Goal: To develop the sound of /s/ the letter c makes in some words.
Procedure:
  1. Have students listen to the /s/ correspondence.
  2. Have the students listen to the /s/ in the following words (you may want to remind students that the c can also stand for the /k/ as in cat, can, etc., but in these words the c makes the /s/):
     cent
     city
     cider
     circle
     cement
     center

Guide pupils to blend onset and rime with the correspondence words:

(onset)	(rime)	
/ s /	/ent/ -	cent
/ s/	/i/ /ty/ -	city
/ s/	/i/ /der/ -	cider

Activities:

Rhyme: Introduce the rhyme, "A Sailor Went to Sea" (Appendix B). Students repeat the rhyme with the teacher.

Segmentation: Using a rubber band explain the concept of "stretch".

Teacher Models:
- Using a rubber band show how to stretch a word as the word is said: /sssss/eeeee -/nnnnn-/ttttt/.
- Bring the rubber band back to its original length and says the word fast-Cent!
- Students and teacher continue with this process with the rest of the words that began with the /s/.

Segmentation and Blending

The teacher tells the students, "We are going to play the game 'slow and fast'."

The teacher pronounces the sounds individually very slowly in a word and asks the students to say the word very fast. For example, tell the students, "I am going to say a word very slowly and then I will say it very fast". Listen: / s/ - / e/ - /n/ - /t/ That is the slow way. I am going to say the word very fast: /sent/. Now I am going to say another word very slowly: / s / - / i / - / t / - /i/. Can you say it fast? city!

Segmentation is the opposite of blending. Stretching the pronunciation of words helps the students hear the separate sounds in a word. The student is blending also in this process. After the students can blend the sounds, the teacher can begin to have the student segment the sounds, too. After students can segment sounds, engage them in blending and segmenting activities by having them say a word very slowly and then saying it fast.

Manipulate the sounds/Substitution

Tell the students, " Listen as I make a new word from ent by changing the /_s/ to an /l/". Can you tell me what the new word is? lent.

Read Aloud

Listening to the reading is a natural way for children to become familiar with how language works. After children have listened to a story, have them go back into the book and find words. Write the words on the board or on a flip chart. Have the children look for the sounds they already know. The more children listen to stories the more they develop sound/letter/word relationship on their own when they read.

Suggested book that supports phonetic elements for the consonant c and the sound of /s/:

Class Alphabet Book
   Add to the class alphabet book the initial consonant sound introduced to the students. The letter and sound in the Class Alphabet Book is the C.

Alphabet Book: C /s/ (sound of the week)
   Give students homework on Monday. Through a newsletter to parents let them know that their child will be studying the sound of the sound of /s/ all week. Tell parents to help their child collect pictures that they will bring to school that begin with c but makes the /s/ sound. Have students paste pictures that begin with the sound /s/ on the C page.

C (e, i, y)

PRACTICE AND REINFORCEMENT ACTIVITIES

(See Appendix A)

The following activities are recommended for each consonant. These activities are described and exemplified in Appendix A.

PHONEMIC AWARENESS UNIT

Goal: To introduce the /j/ sound of *g* correspondence.
Procedure:
   Have students listen to the g = /j/ correspondence.
   Have the students listen to the /j/ in the following words:
      gentle
      gem
      gym
      giraffe
   Blend onset and rime with the correspondence words:
      Onset   +   rime = word
      /j/ g   +   /im/ = gym

Activities:

Explain: When presenting the g /j/, tell students that in some words the letter g can stand for the sound /j/ as in gym or the sound /j/ as in giraffe.

Introduce the rhyme: Students repeat the rhyme with the teacher.

Segmentation: Using a rubber band explain the concept of "stretch".

Teacher Models:
- Using a rubber band show how to stretch a word as the word is said: /jjjjjjjj-/iiiiiiii/-mmmmm/.
- Bring the rubber band back to its original length and says the word fast - /jim/.
- Students and teacher continue with this process with the rest of the /j/ words.

Segmentation and Blending
> The teacher pronounces the sounds individually very slowly in a word and asks the students to say the word very fast. For example, tell the students, "I am going to say a word very slowly and then I will say it very fast". Listen: / j/ - /i / - /m/. That is the slow way. I am going to say the word very fast: /jim/. Now I am going to say another word very slowly: /j/ - /i/ - /a/ - /n/ - /t/. Can you say it fast? giant! Segmentation is the opposite of blending. Stretching the pronunciation of words helps the students hear the separate sounds in a word. The student is blending also in this process. After the students can blend the sounds, the teacher can begin to have the student segment the sounds, too. After students can segment sounds, engage them in blending and segmenting activities by having them say a word slow and then saying it fast.

Manipulate the sounds
> Tell the students, "I can make a new word by changing the // to an //". Can you tell me what the new word is?

Read Aloud
> Listening to the reading is a natural way for children to become familiar with how language works. After children have listened to a story, have them go back into the book and find words. Write the words on the board or a flip chart. Have the children look for the sounds they already know. The more children listen to stories the more they develop sound/letter/word relationship on their own when they read. Suggested book that supports phonetic elements for the consonant g: *The Bee Tree* by Patricia Polacco (Philomel Books, 1993).

Class Alphabet Book
> Begin a class alphabet book with the initial consonants. The first letter and sound in the Class Alphabet Book is the Gg /j/.

Alphabet Book: Gg - /j/
   Give students homework on Monday. Through a newsletter to parents let
   them know that their child will be studying the letter g all week. Tell parents to help their child collect pictures that they will bring to school that
   begin with the g /j/. Have students paste pictures that begin with the
   sound /j/ on the G page.

PRACTICE AND REINFORCEMENT ACTIVITIES

(See Appendix A)

   The activities found in Appendix A are recommended for each consonant. These activities are described and exemplified but can be adapted to
meet the needs of your students.

PHONEMIC AWARENESS UNIT

Goal: To develop the sound of V.
Procedure:
   Have students listen to the /v/ correspondence.
   Have the students listen to the /v / in the following words:
      van
      vet
      vip
      vase
      violin
      vest
   Guide pupils to blend onset and rime with the correspondence words:
      (onset)   (rime)
      / v /   /an/ -   van
      / v/   /et/ -   vet
      /v/   /ip/ -   vip

Activities:

Rhyme: Introduce the rhyme, "Our Van". Students repeat the rhyme with
the teacher.

We have a van,
Our van is very, very nice.
But our van squeaks,
Do you think our van has mice?

Segmentation: Using a rubber band explain the concept of "stretch".

Teacher Models:
- Using a rubber band show how to stretch a word as the word is said: /vvvvvv/ -/aaaaa-/nnnnnnn/.
- Bring the rubber band back to its original length and says the word fast - /van /.
- Students and teacher continue with this process with the rest of the words that began with the /v/.

Segmentation and Blending

The teacher tells the students, "We are going to play the game 'slow and fast'."

The teacher pronounces the sounds individually very slowly in a word and asks the students to say the word very fast. For example, tell the students, "I am going to say a word very slowly and then I will say it very fast". Listen: / v/ - / a/ - /n/. That is the slow way. I am going to say the word very fast: / van /. Now I am going to say another word very slowly: /v / - / e / - / t/. Can you say it fast? vet!

Segmentation is the opposite of blending. Stretching the pronunciation of words helps the students hear the separate sounds in a word. The student is blending also in this process. After the students can blend the sounds, the teacher can begin to have the student segment the sounds, too. After students can segment sounds, engage them in blending and segmenting activities by having them say a word very slowly and then saying it fast.

Manipulate the sounds/Substitution

Tell the students, " Listen as I make a new word from by changing the /v/ to a /p/". Can you tell me what the new word is? pan.

Read Aloud

Listening to the reading is a natural way for children to become familiar with how language works. After children have listened to a story, have them go back into the book and find words. Write the words on the board or a flip chart. Have the children look for the sounds they already know. The more children listen to stories the more they develop sound/letter/word relationship on their own when they read.

Class Alphabet Book

Begin a class alphabet book with the initial consonant sound introduced to the students. The letter and sound in the Class Alphabet Book is the V.

Alphabet Book: V (sound of the week)

Give students homework on Monday. Through a newsletter to parents let them know that their child will be learning the sound of the letter v all week. Tell parents to help their child collect pictures that they will bring to school that begin with the v sound. Have students paste pictures that begin with the sound v on the V page.

PRACTICE AND REINFORCEMENT ACTIVITIES

(See Appendix A)

The activities found in Appendix A are recommended for each consonant. These activities are described and exemplified but can be adapted to meet the needs of your students.

PHONEMIC AWARENESS UNIT

Goal: To introduce the z = /z/ correspondence.
Procedure:
  Have students listen to the z = /z/ correspondence.
  Have the students listen to the /z/ in the following words:
    zoo   zipper   zinnia
    zebra   zucchini
  Blend onset and rime with the correspondence words:
    (onset)   (rime)
    /z/   /oo/ -   /zoo/
    /z/   /per/ -   /ziper/
    /z/   /bra/-   /zebra/

Activities:
  Introduce the rhyme: "The Zigzag Boy and Girl". Students repeat the rhyme with the teacher.

> I know a little zigzag boy
> Who goes this way and that.
> He never knows just where he put
> His coat or shoes or hat.
>
> I know a little zigzag girl
> Who flutters here and there.
> She never knows just where to find
> Her brush to fix her hair.
>
> If you are not a zigzag child
> You'll have no cause to say,
> That you forgot, for you will know
> Where things are put away.

Segmentation: Using a rubber band explain the concept of "stretch".

Teacher Models:
- Using a rubber band show how to stretch a word as the word is said: /zzzzzzzz/-/ooooooooo/.
- Bring the rubber band back to its original length and says the word fast - /zoo/.
- Students and teacher continue with this process with the rest of the /z/ words.

Segmentation and Blending

The teacher pronounces the sounds individually very slowly in a word and asks the students to say the word very fast. For example, tell the students, "I am going to say a word very slowly and then I will say it very fast". Listen: /z/ - /e/ - /br/ - /a/. That is the slow way. I am going to say the word very fast: /zebra/. Now I am going to say another word very slowly: /z/ - /i/ - /p/ - /er/. Can you say it fast? zipper! Segmentation is the opposite of blending. Stretching the pronunciation of words helps the students hear the separate sounds in a word. The student is blending also in this process. After the students can blend the sounds, the teacher can begin to have the student segment the sounds, too. After students can segment sounds, engage them in blending and segmenting activities by having them say a word slow and then saying it fast.

Manipulate the sounds

Tell the students, "I can make a new word from zoo by changing the /z/ to a /t/". Can you tell me what the new word is? too.

Read Aloud

Listening to the reading is a natural way for children to become familiar with how language works. After children have listened to a story, have them go back into the book and find words. Write the words on the board or a flip chart. Have the children look for the sounds they already know. The more children listen to stories

Suggested book that supports phonetic elements for the consonant z: *To the Zoo: Animal Poems* selected by Lee Bennett Hopkins (Little, Brown, 1992).

Class Alphabet Book

Begin a class alphabet book with the initial consonants. The first letter and sound in the Class Alphabet Book is the Zz /z/.

Alphabet Book is the Zz /z/

Give students homework on Monday. Through a newsletter to parents let them know that their child(ren) will be learning the sound of the letter Zz all week. Tell parents to help their child(ren) collect pictures that they will bring to school that begin with the z /z/. Have students paste pictures that begin with the sound /z/ on the Z page.

PRACTICE AND REINFORCEMENT ACTIVITIES

(See Appendix A)

The activities found in Appendix A are recommended for each consonant. These activities are described and exemplified but can be adapted to meet the needs of your students.

PHONEMIC AWARENESS UNIT

Goal: To introduce the qu = /kw/ correspondence.
Procedure:
Have students listen to the qu = /kw/ correspondence.
Have the students listen to the /kw/ in the following words:

queen	quack
quick	quit

Blend onset and rime with the correspondence words:

(onset)	(rime)	
/kw/	/een/ -	/kween/
/kw/	/ick/ -	/kwick/
/kw/	/ack/ -	/kwack/

Activities:
Introduce the rhyme: "Engine, Engine, Number Nine" (page 106, Appendix B). Students repeat the rhyme with the teacher.

Segmentation: Using a rubber band explain the concept of "stretch".

Teacher Models:
- Using a rubber band show how to stretch a word as the word is said: /kw/-/a/-/ck/.
- Bring the rubber band back to its original length and says the word fast - /kwack/.
- Students and teacher continue with this process with the rest of the /kw/ words.

Segmentation and Blending
The teacher pronounces the sounds individually very slowly in a word and asks the students to say the word very fast.

Procedure
1. Tell the students, "I am going to say a word very slowly and then I will say it very fast".

2. Listen: /kw/ /kw/ /kw/ - /i / /i/ /i/ - /ck/ /ck/ /ck/. This is the slow way.
3. Listen: Now, I am going to say the word very fast: /kwick/.
4. I am going to say another word very slowly: /kw/ - /a/ - /ck/.
5. Can you say it fast? quack!
6. Continue with this process with the rest of the qu words.

Segmentation is the opposite of blending. Segmentation is stretching the pronunciation of words to help the students hear the separate sounds in the word. The student learns to blend the stretched out sounds in this process. After the students can blend the segmented sounds, the teacher can begin to have the student segment the sounds and then to blend them. After students can segment sounds, engage them in blending and segmenting activities by having them say a word slow and then saying it fast.

Sound Substitution or Manipulating the Sounds

Procedure
1. Tell the students, "I can make a new word from quack by changing the /kw/ to a /t/".
2. If I change the qu to a t what is the new word ? (tack.)
3. If I change the t to an l what is the new word? (lack)
4. If I use the beginning sound in Matts, name and add –ack, what is the new word? (mack)
5. Continue with this process with other beginning sounds. (r, s, p, b)

Read Aloud

Listening to the reading is a natural way for children to become familiar with how language works. After children have listened to a story, have them go back into the book and find words. Write the words on the board or a flip chart. Have the children look for the sounds they already know. The more children listen to stories the more they develop sound/letter/word relationship on their own when they read. Suggested book that supports phonetic elements for the consonant qu: *The Missing Tarts*, by B.G. Hennessy (Viking Kestrel, 1989).

Class Alphabet Book

Begin a class alphabet book with the initial consonants. The first letter and sound in the Class Alphabet Book is the Qu /kw/.

Alphabet Book: Qu - /kw/

Give students homework on Monday. Through a newsletter to parents let them know that their child(ren) will be studying the letter Qu all week. Tell parents to help their child(ren) collect pictures that they will bring to school that begin with the qu /kw/. Have students paste pictures that begin with the sound /kw/ on the Qu page.

PRACTICE AND REINFORCEMENT ACTIVITIES

(See Appendix A)

The activities found in Appendix A are recommended for each consonant. These activities are described and exemplified but can be adapted to meet the needs of your students.

PHONEMIC AWARENESS UNIT

Goal: To develop the sounds the x makes (/z/ ; /ks/)
Procedure:
Have students listen to the /z/ & /ks/ correspondence. The letter x does not appear frequently as an initial consonant, but it is important to introduce it for the sake of completeness.
Have the students listen to the /z / & /ks/ in the following words:

xylophone-	/z/
x-ray -	/ks/
box =	/ks/

Read Aloud
Listening to the reading is a natural way for children to become familiar with how language works. After children have listened to a story, have them go back into the book and find words. Write the words on the board or a flip chart. Have the children look for the sounds they already know. The more children listen to stories the more they develop sound/letter/word relationship on their own when they read.

Suggested book that supports phonetic elements for the consonant x and the sounds of /x/ and /ks/: *Book Title*, by Author's name (Publisher, year).

Class Alphabet Book
Begin a class alphabet book with the initial consonant sound introduced to the students. The letter and sound in the Class Alphabet Book is the X.

Alphabet Book: /z/ and /ks/ (sounds of the week)
Give students homework on Monday. Through a newsletter to parents let them know that their child will be learning the sound the X makes all week. Tell parents to help their child collect pictures that they will bring

to school that begin with the X (/z/ & /ks/ sounds. Have students paste pictures that begin with the sound /z/ and the /ks/ on the X page.

PRACTICE AND REINFORCEMENT ACTIVITIES

(See Appendix A)

The activities found in Appendix A are recommended for each consonant. These activities are described and exemplified but can be adapted to meet the needs of your students.

References

Adams, Marilyn Jager (1990). Beginning to Read: Thinking and Learning about Print. Cambridge, MA: MIT Press.

Adams, M.J.; Foorman, Barbara R.; Lundberg, Ingvar; and Beeler, Terri (1998). Phonemic Awareness in Young Children. Paul H. Brooks Publishing.

Beaty, Janice J. (1994). Observing Development of the Young Child. Merrill Publishing.

Canter, A Sylvan Learning Company, (1999). Strategies for Teaching Reading: Grades K–6. Santa Monica, CA: Canter and Associates, Inc.

Chard, D.J. and Dickson, S.V. (1999). "Phonological Awareness: Instructional and Assessment Guidelines." http://www.ldonline.org/article/6254.

Edelen-Smith, Patricia J. (2003). Learning First Alliance.

Elkonin, D.B. (1973). "Reading in the USSR." In J. Dowing (ed.), Comparative reading (pp. 551–579). New York: Macmillan.

Gentry, R. (1997). My Kid Can't Spell. Portsmouth, NH: Heinemann.

Griffith, Priscilla, and Mary W. Olson (1992). "Phonemic Awareness Helps Beginning Readers Break the Code." Reading Teacher, 45 (7), 516–523.

Griffith, Priscilla, et al. (1992). "The Effect of Phonemic Awareness on the Literacy Development of First Grade Children in a Traditional or a Whole Language Classroom." Journal of Research in Childhood Education, 6(2), 85–92.

Gunning, Thomas, G. (2000). Phonological Awareness and Primary Phonics. Allyn and Bacon.

Hall, S.H. and Moats, L.C. (1999). Straight Talk about Reading: How Parents Can Make a Difference during the Early Years. Chicago: Contemporary Books.

International Reading Association Board of Directors Position Paper. (1998). IRA, Newark, Delaware. www.reading.org.

National Institute of Literacy, http://www.nifl.gov.

National Reading Panel. (2000). Teaching Children to Read: An Evidence-Based Assessment of the Scientific Research Literature on Reading and Its Implications for

Reading Instruction. Washington, DC: U.S. Department of Health and Human Services. http://www.nationalreadingpanel.org.

Nicholson, T. (1999). "Literacy in the family and society." In G.B. Thompson and T. Nicholson (eds.). Learning to Read: Beyond Phonics and Whole Language (pp. 1–22). Newark, DE: International Reading Association.

O'Conner, Notari-Syverson, and Vadasey (1998). "Ladder to Literacy.

Piaget, Jean. (n.d.). Theory of Cognitive Development. http://en.wikipedia.org/wiki/

Read, C. (1979). "Pre-school Children's Knowledge of English Phonology." *Harvard Educational Review*, 41,1–34.

Snow, Burns, & Griffin, (1998). Preventing Reading Difficulties in Young Children. Washington, DC: National Academy Press.

Stanovich, Keith E. (1986). Matthew Effects in Reading: Some Consequences of Individual Differences in the Acquisition of Literacy. *Reading Research Quarterly*, 21, 360–406.

Stanovich, Keith E. (1993–1994). "Romance and Reality (Distinguished Educator Series)." *Reading Teacher*, 47(4), 280–291.

Temple, Charles; Ogle, Donna; Crawford, Alan; Freppon, Penny. (2008). All Children Read: Teaching for Literacy in Today's Diverse Classrooms (2nd ed.). Allyn and Bacon.

Torgesen, J.K.; Wagner, R.K.; and Rashoote, C.A. (1994). "Longitudinal studies of phonological processing and reading." *Journal of Learning Disabilities*, 27, 276–286.

Trieman, Rebecca (1985). "Onsets and Rimes as Units of Spoken Syllables: Evidence from Children." *Journal of Experimental Child Psychology*, 39, 161–181.

Watson, R.L. (1984). "Scheme and Point in Pacoh Expository Discourse." In Robert El Longacre (ed.), Theory and Application in Processing Text in Non-Indoeuropean Language. Hamburg: Buske.

Wylie, R. E. and Durrell, D.D. (1970). Teaching Vowels Through Phonograms. *Elementary English Journal*, 47, 787–791.

Yopp, Hallie Kay (1992). "Developing Phonemic Awareness in Young Children." *Reading Teacher*, 45 (9), 696–703.

Yopp, Hallie Kay (1995). "A Test for Assessing Phonemic Awareness in Young Children." *Reading Teacher*, 49 (1), 20–29.

Appendix A

Practice and Reinforcement Activities

The activities are recommended for each consonant. These activities are described and exemplified but can be adapted to meet the needs of your students.

Activities to develop rhyming, sound substitution, sound isolation, segmentation, segmentation and blending are described in this section. The teacher can adapt activities to align them to the age or grade level of children. These activities are designed to be fun and interactive to allow all children to participate.

1. Snap and Clap Rhymes.
    Begin with a simple clap and snap rhythm.

    | Clap | Clap | Snap | fall | Clap | Clap | Snap | ball |
    | Clap | Clap | Snap | hall | Clap | Clap | Snap | small |

    A variation is the "I say, You say" activity:
    I say cat. You say _____.   I say pet. You say _____.

2. Rhyming Word Sit Down.
    Children walk around in a big circle taking one step each time a rhyming word is said by the teacher.
    When the teacher says a word that does not rhyme, the children sit down:

    she   tree   flea   spree   key   bee   sea   went

3. Rhyming words in songs, poems, and big books.
    As you do shared reading with the students, pause at the end of phrases and let the students supply the rhyming words.
    After you have read the poem together ask students to find the rhyming words.

Generate other words that rhyme with these rhyming words.

4. Syllable Clap.
   Clap for each syllable in a word or a student's name.
   Example:

Joe	1 Clap
Mandy	2 Claps
Mirasol	3 Claps

5. Syllable Count: Cookie Sheet and Tokens.
   Use tokens to count for each syllable in a word.
   Provide students with cookie sheet and 3 tokens. They push a token forward for each syllable they hear in the word you say.

Pat	1 token
Cake	1 token
Football	2 tokens

6. Rhyming Riddles using Onset and Rime.
   Asking children riddles that require them to manipulate sounds in their heads.

   1. The easiest are the ones that ask for ending.
   2. The next easiest are the ones that ask for a single consonant substitution at the beginning.
   3. The most difficult are the ones that ask for a consonant blend or digraph at the beginning.

   Example: change the word in bold and the sound /d/ to fit the lesson.

   What rhymes with (pig) and starts with /d/? dig
   What rhymes with book and starts with /c/? cook
   What rhymes with sing and starts with /r/? ring
   What rhymes with dog and starts with /fr/? frog

7. Songs that Teach Sound Substitution.
   Example: Choose a song your students all know and substitute a consonant sound for the beginning of each word in the song. One song that is recommended because it works well is from "I've Been working on the Railroad" (Yopp, 1992)

   Fee –Fi—Fiddle-ee-I-Oh
   Bee-Bi-Biddle-ee-I-Oh
   Dee-Di-Diddle-ee-I-Oh
   Hee-Hi-Hiddle-ee-I-Oh

   Old MacDonald Had a Farm can be used . Make substitutions when singing about each animal (Yopp, 1992).

8. Stretchy Names and Stretchy Words.

   Students and teacher clap and say a verse for each child in the class: Example:

   Maggie, Maggie, How do you do? Who's that friend right next to you?

   Students and teacher say the next child's name very slowly, stretching palms far apart as the word is stretched: RRR-eeee-bbbb-eee, ckck-ckck-aaa.

   Clap once quickly and say the name fast: Rebecca.

9. Elkonin Boxes or Sound Boxes.

   Provide each student with Elkonin Sound Boxes on their paper or lapboards. See Figure 2.1: Elkonin Sound Boxes for instructions on how to prepare sound boxes for each student.

   Elkonin Sound Boxes help children learn to listen to the sounds in a word, say a word, stretching it out so that each sound is heard, and then slide a token into each box as they hear each sound.

   Continue with other words that have 2 or 3 phonemes.

10. A Song to Teach Phonemic Segmentation.

    Listen, listen to my word,

    Then tell me all the sound you heard: race

    /r/ is one sound
    /a/ is two,
    /s/ is last in race it's true
    Thanks for listening to my word
    And telling all the sounds you heard!

Appendix B

Literary Selections

Rhymes and songs that can be used to reinforce phonemic awareness.

A

A-Hunting We Will Go

A-hunting we will go,
A-hunting we will go.
We'll catch a fox
And put him in a box.
And then we'll let him go.

B

Baa, Baa, Black Sheep

Baa, baa, black sheep,
Have you any wool?
Yes, sir, yes, sir, Three bags full.
One for the master,
One for the dame,
But none for the little boy
Who cries in the lane.

The Balloon

What is the news of the day, my good
Mr. Gray?
They say the balloon
Has gone up to the moon.

The Bear Went over the Mountain

The bear went over the mountain,
The bear went over the mountain,
The bear went over the mountain,
To see what he could see.

Bedtime

  Down with the lambs
    Up with the lark,
  Run to bed, children,
    Before it gets dark.

Bees

If bees stay at home,
Rain will soon come.
If they fly away,
Fine will be the day.

Bingo

There was a farm-er who had a dog.
And Bing-o was his name-o.
B-I-N-G-O, B-I-N-G-O, B-I-N-G-O,
And Bing-o was his name-o.

Bow, Wow, Wow

Bow, wow, wow,
Whose dog art thou?
Little Tom Tinker's dog,
Bow, wow, wow.

The Boy in the Barn

A little boy went into a barn,
And lay down on some hay.
An owl came out, and flew about,
And the little boy ran away.

Burnie Bee

Burnie bee, burnie bee,
Tell me when your wedding be?
If it be tomorrow day,
Take your wings and fly away.

C

Clouds

Christina Rossetti

White sheep, white sheep,
On a blue hill,
When the wind stops,
You all stand still.
When the wind blows,
You walk away slow.
White sheep, white sheep,
Where do you go?

Come on In

Come on in, The water's fine. I'll give you Till I count to nine. If you're
not hi by then, Guess I'll have to Count to ten.

D

Dickery, Dickery, Dare

Dickery, dickery, dare,
The pig flew up in the air;
The man in brown
Soon brought him down,
Dickery, dickery, dare.

Did You Ever See a Lassie?

Did you ever see a lassie, a lassie, a lassie,
Did you ever see a lassie go this way and that,
Go this way and that way and this way and that way?
Did you ever see a lassie go this way and that?

The Donkey

Donkey, donkey, old and gray,
Open your mouth and gently bray;
Lift your ears and blow your horn,
To wake the world this sleepy morn.

E

Engine, Engine, Number Nine

Engine, Engine, Number Nine,
Running on the Chicago line.
See it sparkle, see it shine,
Engine, Engine, Number Nine.

F

The Farmer in the Dell

The farm-er in the dell,
The farm-er in the dell,
Heigh-ho the der-ry-o,
The farm-er in the dell.
The farm-er takes a wife.
The farm-er takes a wife.
Heigh-ho the der-ry-o,
The farm-er takes a wife.

Fears and Tears

Tommy's tears and Mary's fears
Will make them old
Before their years.

Fire! Fire!

"Fire! Fire!" said Mrs. McGuire.
"Where? Where?" said Mrs. Hare.
"Downtown!" said Mrs. Brown.
"Heaven save us!" said Mrs. Davis.

Fishy-fishy

Fishy-fishy in the brook,
Daddy caught him with a hook.
Mama fried him in the pan,
And baby ate him like a man.

Five Little Ducks

Five little ducks went out one day,
Over the hills and far away.
One little duck went

"Quack, quack, quack."
Four little ducks came swimming back.

Four little ducks went out one day,
Over the hills and far away.
One little duck went
"Quack, quack, quack."
Three little ducks came swimming back.

Three little ducks went out one day,
Over the hills and far away.
One little duck went
"Quack, quack, quack."
Two little ducks came swimming back.

Two little ducks went out one day,
Over the hills and far away.
One little duck went
"Quack, quack, quack."
One little duck came swimming back.

Five Miles from Home

(sung to tune of "The Farmer in the Dell")
We're five miles from home.
We're five miles from home.
We sing a-while and talk a-while,
We're four miles from home.
We're four miles from home.
We're four miles from home.
We sing a-while and talk a-while,
We're three miles from home.
We're three miles from home, etc.
We're two miles from home, etc.
We're one mile from home.
We're one mile from home.
We sing a-while and talk a-while,
And now we're at home.

Fooba Wooba John

Saw a flea kick a tree,
Fooba wooba, fooba wooba,
Saw a flea kick a tree,
Fooba wooba, John.
Saw a flea kick a tree

In the middle of the sea,
Fooba wooba, fooba wooba,
Fooba wooba John.
Saw a crow flying low,
Fooba wooba, fooba wooba,

Saw a crow flying low,
Fooba wooba John.
Saw a crow flying low,
Miles and miles beneath the snow,
Fooba wooba, fooba wooba,
Fooba wooba John.

Saw a bug give a shrug . . .
In the middle of the rug . . .
Saw a whale chase a snail . . .
All around a water pail . . .
Saw two geese making cheese . . .
One would hold and the other would squeeze.
Saw a mule teaching school . . .
To some bullfrogs in the pool . . .
Saw a bee off to sea . . .
With his fiddle across his knee . . .
Saw a hare chase a deer . . .
Ran it all of seven year . . .
Saw a bear scratch his ear . . .
Wonderin' what we're doin' here.

Fright and Bright

Poor Cat Fright
Ran off with all her might
Because the dog was after her—Poor Cat Fright!
Poor Dog Bright
Ran off with all his might
Because the cat was after him.
Poor Dog Bright!

Fuzzy Wuzzy

Fuzzy Wuzzy was a bear.
Fuzzy Wuzzy had no hair.
Fuzzy Wuzzy wasn't fuzzy, Was he?

G

Garden Gate

Two, four, six, eight.
Meet me at the garden gate.
If I'm late, do not wait.
Two, four, six, eight.

The Gingerbread Man

Smiling girls, rosy boys,
Come and buy my little toys;
Monkeys made of gingerbread,
And sugar horses painted red.

Go and Tell Aunt Nancy

Go and tell Aunt Nancy,
Go and tell Aunt Nancy,
Go and tell Aunt Nancy,
    The old gray goose is dead.

The one that she was saving,
The one that she was saving,
The one that she was saving,
To make a feather bed.
She died on Friday,
She died on Friday,
She died on Friday,
    Behind the old barn shed.
She left nine little goslings,
She left nine little goslings,
She left nine little goslings,
    To scratch for their own bread.

Go In and Out the Window

Go in and out the win-dow,
Go in and out the win-dow,
Go in and out the win-dow,
As we have done be-fore.

Go to Bed Late

Go to bed late,
Stay very small.
Go to bed early,
Grow very tall.

The Goat

There was a man—now please take note—
There was a man who had a goat.
He loved that goat—indeed he did—
He loved that goat just like a kid.

One day that goat felt frisky and fine,
Ate three red shirts from off the line.
The man, he grabbed him by the back,
And tied him to a railroad track.

But when the train drove into sight,
The goat grew pale and green with fright.
He heaved a sigh as if in pain,
Coughed up those shirts, and flagged the train.

Gobble, Gobble

A turkey is a funny bird,
His head goes wobble, wobble,
And he knows just one word,
Gobble, gobble, gobble.

Good, Better, Best

Good, better, best,
Never let it rest,
Till your good is better
And your better best.

H

Happy Thought

Robert Louis Stevenson

The world is so full, of a number of things, I'm sure we should all be as
happy as kings.

Hey Diddle, Diddle

Hey diddle, diddle,
The cat and the fiddle,

The cow jumped over the moon.
The little dog laughed
To see such a sport,
And the dish ran away with the spoon.

Help! Murder! Police!

Help! Murder! Police!
My mother fell in the grease.
I laughed so hard, I fell in the lard.
Help! Murder! Police!
Hiccup, hiccup
Hiccup, hiccup, go away!
Come again another day.
Hiccup, hiccup, when I bake,
I'll give to you a butter-cake.

Hickory, Dickory, Dock

Hickory, dickory, dock,
The mouse ran up the clock.
The clock struck one,
The mouse ran down!
Hickory, dickory, dock.

Higher Than a House

Higher than a house,
Higher than a tree,
Oh! Whatever can that be?

Hippity Hop to the Barber Shop

Hippity hop to the barber shop,
To get a stick of candy,
One for you and one for me,
And one for sister Mandy.

Hot Boiled Beans

Boys and girls come to supper—
Hot boiled beans
And very good butter.

Hot Cross Buns!

Hot cross buns! Hot cross buns!
One a penny, two a penny,
Hot cross buns!
If you have no daughters,

Give them to your sons;
One a penny, two a penny,
Hot cross buns!

I

I Asked My Mother for Fifteen Cents

I asked my mother for fifteen cents
To see the elephant jump the fence,
He jumped so high he touched the sky
And never came back 'till the Fourth of July.

I Saw Esau

I saw Esau sawing wood,
And Esau saw I saw him;
Though Esau saw I saw him saw,
Still Esau went on sawing.

I Saw Three Ships

I saw three ships come sail-ing by,
Come sail-ing by, come sail-ing by,
I saw three ships come sail-ing by,
On New Year's Day, in the morn-ing.

Ice Cream Rhyme

I scream, you scream,
We all scream for ice cream.

If You Ever

If you ever ever ever ever,
If you ever ever ever ever meet a whale,
You must never never never never never,
You must never never never never never touch
    its tail,
For if you ever ever ever ever ever,
For if you ever ever ever ever ever touch its tail,
You will never never never never never,
You will never never never never never meet
    another whale.

If You Should Meet a Crocodile

If you should meet a crocodile,
Don't take a stick and poke him;

Ignore the welcome in his smile,
Be careful not to stroke him.
For as he sleeps upon the Nile,
He thinner gets and thinner;
And whene'er you meet a crocodile,
He's ready for his dinner.

If You're Happy and You Know It

If you're hap-py and you know it,
Clap your hands.
If you're hap-py and you know it,
Clap your hands.
If you're hap-py and you know it,
And you really want to show it,
If you're hap-py and you know it,
Clap your hands.

I'll Sing You a Song

I'll sing you a song,
Though not very long,
Yet I think it as pretty as any.

Put your hand in your purse,
You'll never be worse,
And give the poor singer a penny.

I'm a Little Teapot

I'm a little teapot short and stout:
Here is my handle and here is my spout.
When I get all steamed up, I just shout:
"Just tip me over and pour me out!"

It Ain't Going to Rain No More

It ain't going to rain no more, no more,
It ain't going to rain no more;
How in the heck can I wash my neck
If it ain't going to rain no more?

It's Raining, It's Pouring

It's raining, it's pouring,
The old man is snoring.
He went to bed and bumped his head.
And he wouldn't get up in the morning.

I've Been Working on the Railroad

I've been work-ing on the rail-road,
All the live long day,
I've been work-ing on the rail-road,
Just to pass the time a-way.
Don't you hear the whistle blowing?
Rise up so early in the morn.
Don't you hear the cap-tain shout-ing,
"Di-nah, blow your horn!"
Di-nah, won't you blow,
Di-nah, won't you blow
Di-nah, won't you blow your horn?

Some-one's in the kitch-en with Dinah,
Some-one's in the kitch-en, I know,
Someone's in the kitch-en with Dinah,
Strum-ming on the old ban-jo, and sing-ing:
Fee-fi-fidd-lee-i-o
Fee-fi-fidd-lee-i-o, Fee-fi-fidd-lee-i-o,
Strum-ming on the old ban-jo.

I've Got a Dog

I've got a dog as thin as a rail,
He's got fleas all over his tail;
Every time his tail goes flop,
The fleas on the bottom all hop to the top.

J

Jack and Jill

Jack and Jill went up the hill,
To fetch a pail of water,
Jack fell down and broke his crown,
And Jill came tumbling after.

Jack, Be Nimble

Jack, be nimble
Jack, be quick,
Jack, jump over the candlestick.
Jump it lively, Jump it quick, But don't knock over the candlestick.

Jack Hall

Jack Hall, He is so small, A rat could eat him, Hat and all.

Jack Sprat

Jack Sprat could eat no fat,
His wife could eat no lean.
And between them both, you see,
—They licked the platter clean.

Jumping Joan

Here am I, Little Jumping Joan;
When nobody's with me I'm all alone.

L

Lazy Mary

La-zy Mar-y, will you get up,
Will you get up,
will you get up?
La-zy Mar-y, will you get up,
Will you get up to-day?

Oh, no, moth-er, I won't get up,
I won't get up, I won't get up.
Oh, no, moth-er, I won't get up,
I won't get up to-day.

Let's Be Merry

Christina Rossetti

Mother shake the cherry-tree,
　Susan catch a cherry;
　Oh how funny that will be,
　Let's be merry!
　One for brother, one for sister,
　Two for mother more,
　Six for father, hot and tired,
　Knocking at the door.

Little Betty Blue

Little Betty Blue,
Lost her new shoe.
What will poor Betty do?
Why, give her another,
To match the other,
And then she will walk in two.

The Little Bird

Once I saw a little bird
Come hop, hop, hop;
So I cried, "Little bird,
Will you stop, stop, stop?"
I was going to the window
To say, "How do you do?"
But he shook his little tail,
And far away he flew.

Little Blue Ben

Little Blue Ben, who lives in the glen,
Keeps a blue cat and one blue hen,
Which lays of blue eggs a score and ten;
Where shall I find the little Blue Ben?

Little Bo-Peep

Little Bo-Peep has lost her sheep,
And can't tell where to find them;
Leave them alone,
And they'll come home,
Wagging their tails behind them.

Little Boy Blue

Little boy blue, come blow your horn;
The sheep's in the meadow, the cow's in the corn.
Where is the little boy who looks after the sheep?
He's under the haystack fast asleep.
Will you wake him? No, not I;
For if I do, he's sure to cry.

Little Girl, Little Girl, Where Have You Been?

Little girl, little girl, where have you been?
Gathering roses to give to the Queen.
Little girl, little girl, what gave she you?
She gave me a diamond as big as my shoe.

Little Jack Horner

Little Jack Horner
Sat in a corner,
Eating his Christmas pie;

He put in his thumb,
And pulled out a plum,
And said, "What a good boy am I!"

Little Old Man

A little old man came riding by.
Said I, "Old man, your horse will die."
Said he, "If he dies, I'll tan his skin.
And if he lives, I'll ride him again."

The Little Plant

Kate L. Brown

In the heart of a seed,
Buried down so deep,
A little plant Lay fast asleep.
"Awake," said the sun,
"Come up through the earth,"
"Awake," said the rain,
"We are giving you birth."
The little plant heard
With a happy sigh,
And pointed its petals
Up to the sky.

Little Puppy Dog

My father owns the butcher shop
My mother cuts the meat,
And I'm the little puppy dog
That runs down the street.

Little Tommy Tucker

Little Tommy Tucker
Sings for his supper. What shall we give him?
White bread and butter. How shall he cut it
Without a knife? How shall he be married
Without a wife?

The Little Turtle

Vachel Lindsey

There was a little turtle.
He lived in a box.

He swam in a puddle.
He climbed on the rocks
He snapped at a mosquito.
He snapped at a flea.
He snapped at a minnow.
And he snapped at me.

Lobby Loo

Here we go lobby loo,
Here we go lobby light.
Here we go lobby loo
All on a Saturday night.

Put your right hand in,
Put your right hand out.
Shake it a little, a little,
And turn yourself about.

Lock and Key

"I am a gold lock."
"I am a gold key."
"I am a silver lock."
"I am a silver key."
"I am a brass lock."
"I am a brass key."
"I am a lead lock."
"I am a lead key."
"I am a don lock."
"I am a don key."

M

Mary's Lamb

Sara Josepha Hale

Mary had a little lamb,
Its fleece was white as snow,
And everywhere that Mary went
The lamb was sure to go.
It followed her to school one day—
That was against the rule,
It made the children laugh and play
To see a lamb at school.

Merrily We Roll Along

Mer-ri-ly we roll a-long, roll a-long, roll a-long,
Mer-ri-ly we roll a-long, o-ver the deep blue sea.

Mix a Pancake

Christina Rossetti

Mix a pancake,
Stir a pancake,
   Pop it in the pan;
Fry a pancake,
Toss the pancake—
   Catch it if you can.

The Mocking Bird

Hush, little baby, don't say a word,
Papa's going to buy you a mocking bird.
If that mocking bird won't sing,
Papa's going to buy you a diamond ring.
If the diamond ring turns to brass,
Papa's going to buy you a looking-glass.
If the looking-glass gets broke,
Papa's going to buy you a billy goat.
If that billy goat runs away,
Papa's going to buy you another today.

The Mulberry Bush

Here we go round the mulberry bush,
   The mulberry bush,
   The mulberry bush,
   Here we go round the mulberry bush,
   On a cold and frosty morning.

This is the way we clap our hands,
   Clap our hands,
   Clap our hands,
This is the way we clap our hands,
On a cold and frosty morning.

My Son John

Deedle, deedle, dumpling, my son John,
Went to bed with his stockings on;
One shoe off, and one shoe on,
Deedle, deedle, dumpling, my son John.

N

The North Wind Doth Blow

The north wind doth blow,
And we shall have snow,
And what will poor Robin do then?
    Poor thing! He'll sit in a barn,
    And keep himself warm,
    And hide his head under his wing.
Poor thing!

O

Oh Where, Oh Where Has My Little Dog Gone?

Oh where, oh where has my little dog gone?
    Oh where, oh where can he be?
    With his ears cut short and his tail cut long
    Oh where, oh where is he?

Old Chairs to Mend

If I'd as much money as I could spend,
I never would cry old chairs to mend;
Old chairs to mend, old chairs to mend,
I never would cry old chairs to mend.

If I'd as much money as I could tell,
I never would cry old clothes to sell;
Old clothes to sell, old clothes to sell;
I never would cry old clothes to sell.

Old King Cole

Old King Cole
Was a merry old soul,
And a merry old soul was he.
He called for his pipe,
And he called for his bowl,
And he called for his fiddlers three.

Old MacDonald

Old MacDonald had a farm, E-I-E-I-O.
And on this farm he had some sheep, E-I-E-I-O.
With a baa-baa here and a baa-baa there,

Here a baa,
there a baa,
ev-ry-where a baa baa,
Old MacDonald had a farm, E-I-E-I-O.

The Old Man of Peru

There was an old man of Peru,
Who dreamt he was eating his shoe.
He woke in the night
In a terrible fright,
And found it was perfectly true.

Old Woman, Old Woman

There was an old woman tossed in a basket,
Seventeen times as high as the moon;
But where she was going no one could tell,
For under her arm she carried a broom.
"Old woman, old woman, old woman," said I,
"Where, oh where, oh where so high?"
"To sweep the cobwebs from the sky;
And I'll be with you by and by."

One for the Money

One for the money,
Two for the show,
Three to make ready,
And four to go.

One, Two, Three, Four, Five

One, two, three, four, five
Once I caught a fish alive,
Six, seven, eight, nine, ten,
Then I let it go again.
Why did you let it go?
Because it bit my finger so.
Which finger did it bite?
The little finger on the right.

Our Van

We have a van,
Our van is very, very nice.
But our van squeaks,
Do you think our van has mice?

Out

Out goes the rat,
Out goes the cat,
Out goes the lady With the big green hat.
Y, O, U spells you;
O, U, T spells out!

Owl

A wise old owl lived in an oak,
The more he heard, the less he spoke.
The less he spoke, the more he heard.
Why aren't we all like that wise old bird?

P

Pat-a-Cake

Pat-a-cake, pat-a-cake, baker's man,
Bake me a cake just as fast as you can.
Pat it and stick it, and mark it with a B
Put it in the oven for baby and me.

Pease Porridge

Pease porridge hot,
Pease porridge cold,
Pease porridge in the pot nine days old.

Polly, Put the Kettle On

Polly, put the kettle on,
Polly, put the kettle on,
Polly, put the kettle on,
And let's drink tea.

Pussy-cat, Pussy-cat

Pussy-cat, pussy-cat, where have you been?
I've been to London to visit the Queen!
Pussy-cat, pussy-cat, what did you there?
I frightened a little mouse under her chair.

R

Rain

Rain on the green grass,
And rain on the tree,
Rain on the house-top,
But not on me.

Rain, Rain, Go Away

Rain, rain, go away,
Come again another day;
Little Raymond wants to play.

Red Sky

Red sky at night,
Sailor's delight;
Red sky in the morning,
Sailor's warning.

Roll Over

Ten men in the bed,
and the lit-tle one said,
"Roll o-ver! Roll o-ver!"
They all rolled o-ver
And one fell out.

Nine men in the bed,
and the lit-tle one said,
"Roll o-ver! Roll o-ver!"
They all rolled o-ver
And one fell out.
[Continue until there is just one left.]
One man in the bed, and the lit-tle one said, "Alone at last!"

Row the Boat

Row, row, row your boat
Gently down the stream,
Merrily, merrily, merrily, merrily,
Life is but a dream.

Rub-a-Dub-Dub

Rub-a-dub-dub,
Three men in a tub,
And who do you think they be?

The butcher, the baker,
The candlestick maker.
Rub-a-dub-dub all three.

S

A Sailor Went to Sea

A sailor went to sea
To see what he could see,
And all that he could see,
Was the sea, sea, sea.

Sing, Sing

Sing, sing,
What shall I sing? The cat's run away
With the pudding string! Do, do,
What shall I do? The cat's run away with the pudding, too.

She'll Be Comin' 'Round the Mountain

She'll be corn-in' 'round the moun-tain when she comes,
She'll be com-in' 'round the moun-tain when she comes,
She'll be com-in' 'round the moun-tain,
She'll be com-in' 'round the moun-tain,
She'll be com-in' 'round the moun-tain when she comes.

She'll be driv-in' six white hor-ses when she comes,
She'll be driv-in' six white hor-ses when she comes,
She'll be driv-in' six white hor-ses,
She'll be driv-in' six white hor-ses,
She'll be driv-in' six white hor-ses when she comes.

Oh, we'll all go out to meet her when she comes,
Yes, we'll all go out to meet her when she comes,
Oh, we'll all go out to meet her,
Yes, we'll all go out to meet her,
We will all go out to meet her when she comes.

Simple Simon

Simple Simon met a pieman
   Going to the fair.
   Says Simple Simon to the pieman,
   "Let me taste your ware.
   " Says the pieman to Simple Simon,
   "Show me first your penny.
   " Says Simple Simon to the pieman,
   "Indeed I have not any."

Skip to My Lou

Lost my part-ner, what'll I do?
Lost my part-ner, what'll I do?
Lost my part-ner, what'll I do?
Skip to my Lou, my dar-ling.

Star Light, Star Bright

Star light, star bright,
First star I see tonight,
I wish I may,
I wish I might
Have the wish I wish tonight.

A Sunshiny Shower

A sunshiny shower
Won't last half an hour.

Swim, Swan, Swim

Swan swam over the sea,
   Swim, swan, swim!
   Swan swam back again,
   Well swum, swan!

Swing, Swing

William Allingham

   Swing, swing,
   Sing, sing,
   Here! my throne and I am a king!
   Swing, sing,
   Swing, sing,
   Farewell, earth, for I'm on the wing.

   Low, high,
   Here I fly,
   Like a bird through sunny sky!
   Free, free,
   Over the lea,
   Over the mountain, over the sea!

   Soon, soon,
   Afternoon,

Over the sunset, over the moon!
Far, far,
Over all bar,
Sweeping on from star to star!

No, no,
Low, low.
Sweeping daisies with my toe!
Slow, slow,
To and fro,
Slow—
slow—
slow—
slow!

T

Take Me Out to the Ball Game

Take me out to the ball game,
Take me out to the crowd,
Buy me some peanuts and Crack-er Jacks,
I don't care if I ev-er get back,
And it's root, root, root for the home team,
If they don't win, it's a shame,
For it's one, two, three strikes, "You're out!"
At the old ball game.

Teddy Bear, Teddy Bear

Teddy Bear, Teddy Bear, turn around,
Teddy Bear, Teddy Bear, touch the ground.
Teddy Bear, Teddy Bear, read the news,
Teddy Bear, Teddy Bear, shine your shoes.

There Was a Crooked Man

There was a crooked man,
Who walked a crooked mile,
He found a crooked sixpence
Against a crooked stile;
He bought a crooked cat,
Which caught a crooked mouse.
And they all lived together
In a little crooked house.

There Was an Old Woman

There was an old woman
Who lived under a hill.
And if she's not gone
She lives there still.

This Is the Way We Go to School

This is the way we go to school.
Go to school, go to school.
This is the way we go to school,
On a cold and frosty morning.

Three Blind Mice

Three blind mice, three blind mice,
See how they run, see how they run.
They all ran after the farmer's wife,
Who cut off their tails with the carving knife.
Did you ever see such a sight in your life,
As three blind mice?

Three Little Bugs

Three little bugs in a basket,
Hardly room for two.
One like Lee,
one like Linda,
And one that looks like you.

The Three Little Kittens

Eliza Lee Fallen

Three little kittens
Lost their mittens
And they began to cry,
"Oh mother dear,
We sadly fear
Our mittens we have lost."
"Lost your mittens!
You naughty kittens!
Then you shall have no pie!"
"Mee-ow, mee-ow, mee-ow."
"Then, you shall have no pie."

The three little kittens
They found their mittens
And they began to cry,
"Oh mother dear,
See here, see here,
Our mittens we have found."

"Found your mittens,
You good little kittens?
Then you shall have some pie.
Mee-ow, mee-ow,
Then you shall have some pie."

A Tisket, A Tasket

A tis-ket, a tas-ket, a green and yel-low bas-ket,
I wrote a let-ter to my love,
And on the way, I lost it,
I lost it, I lost it,
I lost my yellow basket.

A little laddie picked it up and put it in his pock-et.

Tom, Tom, the Piper's Son

Tom he was a piper's son,
He learned to play when he was young;
But the only tune that he could play was,
"Over the hills and far away."

Now Tom with his pipe made such a noise,
That he pleased all the girls and boys;
And they stopped to hear him play,
"Over the hills and far away."

Turn to the East

Turn to the east,
And turn to the west,
And turn to the one that you love best.

Twinkle, Twinkle, Little Bat

Lewis Carroll

Twinkle, twinkle, little bat!
How I wonder what you're at!
Up above the world you fly,
Like a tea-tray in the sky.
Twinkle, twinkle—

Twinkle, Twinkle, Little Star

Twinkle, twinkle, little star,
How I wonder what you are!
Up above the world so high,
Like a diamond in the sky.

Two Cats of Kilkenny

There were once two cats of Kilkenny.
Each thought there was one cat too many.
So they fought and they fit,
And they scratched and they bit,
Until, except for their nails,
And the tips of their tails,
Instead of two cats, there weren't any.

Two Little Blackbirds

Two little blackbirds
Sat upon a hill,
One named Jack,
The other named Jill;
Fly away, Jack,
Fly away, Jill,
Come again, Jack,
Come again, Jill.
Two little blackbirds
Sitting on a hill.

U

Up, Dear Children

Come, my dear children,
Up is the sun,
Birds are all singing,
And morn has begun.
Up from the bed,
Miss Out on the lea;
The horses are waiting
For you and for me!

W

Way Down South Where Bananas Grow

Way down South where bananas grow,
A grasshopper stepped on an elephant's toe.

The elephant said, with tears in his eyes,
"Pick on somebody your own size!"

Wee Willie Winkie

Wee Willie Winkie runs through the town,
Upstairs and downstairs in his nightgown,
Rapping at the window, crying through the lock,
Are the children all in bed, for now it's eight o'clock?

What Animals Say

Bow-wow, says the dog,
Mew, mew, says the cat,
Grunt, grunt, goes the hog,
And squeak goes the rat.

Tu-whoo, says the owl,
Caw, caw, says the crow,
Quack, quack, says the duck,
What cuckoos say you know.

What Are Little Boys Made Of?

What are little boys made of?
  Frogs and snails
  And puppy dogs' tails.
That's what little boys are made of.

What Are Little Girls Made Of?

  Sugar and spice
  And all things nice.
That's what little girls are made of.

What Birds Say

Some birds say, "Cuckoo! Cuckoo!" Some birds say, "Caw! Caw!" What
do you say?

Wheels On the Bus

The wheels on the bus
Go round and round,
Round and round, round and round.
The wheels on the bus
Go round and round,
All over town.

Whistle, Daughter

Whistle, daughter, whistle; whistle, daughter dear. I cannot whistle, mommy; I cannot whistle clear. Whistle, daughter, whistle; whistle for a pound. I cannot whistle, mommy; I cannot make a sound.

Windy Nights

Robert Louis Stevenson

Whenever the moon and stars are set,
    Whenever the wind is high,
All night long in the dark and wet,
    A man goes riding by.
Late in the night when the fires are out,
Why does he gallop and gallop about?

Whenever the trees are crying aloud,
    And ships are tossed at sea,
By, on the highway, low and loud,
    By at the gallop goes he.
By at the gallop he goes, and then,
By he comes back at the gallop again.

Wishes

Said the first little chicken
With a queer little squirm,
"I wish I could find a fat little worm."

Said the second little chicken
With an odd little shrug,
"I wish I could find a fat little slug."

Said the third little chicken
With a sharp little squeal,
"I wish I could find Some nice yellow meal."

"Now see here." said their mother
From the green garden patch.
"If you want any breakfast,
Just come here and SCRATCH!"

Woodchuck

How much wood
Would a woodchuck chuck
If a woodchuck could chuck wood?

Z

The Zigzag Boy and Girl

I know a little zigzag boy
Who goes this way and that.
He never knows just where he put
His coat or shoes or hat.

I know a little zigzag girl
Who flutters here and there.
She never knows just where to find
Her brush to fix her hair.

If you are not a zigzag child
You'll have no cause to say,
That you forgot, for you will know
Where things are put away.

Appendix C

Books That Support Phonetic Elements

Consonants H, L, M
  My Great-Aunt Arizona, Gloria Houston (Harper Collins, 1992)

Consonants W, R, N
  The Car Washing Street, Denise Lewis Patrick (Tambourine Books, 1993)

Consonants G, F, M
  The Bee Tree, Patricia Polacco (Philomel Books, 1993)

Consonants D, V, K
  Ming Lo Moves the Mountain, Arnold Lobel (Greenwillow, 1982)

Consonants Z, J
  To the Zoo: Animal Poems, selected by Lee Bennett Hopkins
    (Little Brown, 1992)

Consonants C, Y, B
  Dragonfly's Tale, Kristina Rodanas (Clarion, 1991)

Consonants P, S, T
  Sohie and Sammy's Library Sleepover, Judith Caseley
    (Greenwillow, 1993)

Consonant Sounds Qu
  The Missing Tarts, B.G. Hennessy (Viking Kestrel, 1989)

Final X
  Fox on Stage, James Marshall (Dial, 1993)

Consonant Blends
  Cactus Hotel, Brenda Z. Guiberson (Henry Holt, 1991)

Appendix D

Websites

The following sites are researched based on content and applicability to the development of phonemic awareness. Some of these websites were reviewed and complied to align with the National Reading Panel (NRP) findings of research-based reading instruction and best practices (Wasburn-Moses, 2006).

Others were reviewed by graduate students enrolled in the graduate reading program under the CoMeT-R project at Our Lady of the Lake University. The websites were reviewed for application to classroom instruction by these graduate students teaching in the area schools under the supervision of the author. The websites selected contain material diversity, a wide range of activities, and are have practical classroom application.

http://www.readwritethink.org/lessons/lesson_view.asp?id=120

http://classroomjc-schools.net/read/Phonemic.htm

http://teams.lacoe.edu/DOCUMENTATION/classrooms/patti/k-1/activities/isolation.html

http://www.mcps.k12.md.us/curriculum/littlekids/archieve/KPtemp_chunkvenn.htm

http://www.sasked.gov.sk.ca/docs/ela/e_literacy/awareness.html

http://wik.ed.uiuc.edu/index.php/Phonemic_awareness

http://www.readingrockets.org/article/388

http://www.literatureforliterature.ecsd.net/phonemic_awareness.htm

http://www.manatee.k12.fl.us/sites/elementary/palmasola/rcompindex1.htm

http://www.readwritethink.org

http://www.teams.locoe.edu/documentation/classrooms/patti/k-1/activities/
phonemic.html

http://www.songsforteaching.com/avni/alliterativebooks.html

http://www.getreadytoread.org

http://www.iusd.k12.ca.us/parent_resources/phonemicawareness456.htm

http://www.nationalreadingpanel.org/Publications/publications.htm

http://www.manatee.k12.fl.us/sites/elementary/palmasola/Whereisthesound
index.htm

http://www.tampareads.com/phonics/whereis/index.htm

Appendix E

English and Spanish Form Letters

Date

Dear Parents,

We have learned that when young children work with the sounds of words and understand that words are made up of individual sounds, they learn to read sooner and will become better readers.

Your child will be studying the sounds of letters of the alphabet in our phonemic awareness program. Each week they will study a different letter. You can help your child to become a successful reader by helping him/her collect pictures that he/she will bring to school each Monday. You will be notified of the letter your child will be studying that week.

The objective of this project is for the children in the class to put together an Alphabet Big Book. The Big Book will be used to review the sound and letter that was learned.

You are invited to come and join us during our phonemic awareness class instruction.

Respectfully,

SPANISH

Estimados padres,

Hemos aprendido que cuando los niños estudian los sonidos de las palabras y entienden que las palabras se componen de sonidos individuales, ellos aprenden a leer más pronto y llegan a ser mejores lectores.

Su niño estará estudiando los sonidos de cartas del alfabeto en nuestro programa Fonético de Conocimiento. Cada semana la clase estudiara una letra diferente. Usted puede ayudar a su niño juntar retratos que el/ella traerá a la clase cada lunes que comienza con la letra que estudiarán esa semana. El propósito de este proyecto es para que los niños hagan un libro alfabético para la clase.

Respetuosamente,

Appendix F

Common Phonogram Patterns or Rimes

Syllables can be broken into smaller units called onsets and rimes (Trieman, 1985). The onset is the initial consonant sound of a syllable if there is one; and the rime is the vowel plus any consonant sound that comes after it. Rimes are also referred to as phonogram patterns. They are the rhyming portions of families of words such as the *at* in cat, mat, and pat. In these words *at* is the rime. Rimes are also known as phonogram patterns. Wylie and Durrell (1970) found a group of thirty-seven phonogram patterns that make up many hundreds of English words. The following list is provided for your use:

Phonogram Patterns or Rimes

Back	Meat	Nice	Clock	Duck
Mail	Bell	Stick	Joke	Rug
Rain	Crest	Wide	Shop	Jump
Cake		Light	Store	junk
Sale		Ill	Not	
Game		Win		
Plan		Line		
Bank		Bring		
Trap		Think		
Crash		Trip		
Cat		Fit		
Plate				
Saw				
Stay				

(Temple et al., 2008, p. 78).